THE
Retirement
Obsession

Stop Worrying
& Start Planning
Your Perfect Retirement

Stephen A. Oliver

The Retirement Obsession
Stop Worrying & Start Planning Your Perfect Retirement

Disclaimer

This book is for informational purposes only, is not intended to be a substitute for specific professional financial, tax or legal advice, and does not constitute an offer to sell or a solicitation of an offer to buy any security which may be referenced herein. We suggest that you consult with your financial, tax advisor, or legal professional with regard to your individual situation.

The information within this publication is based on sources believed to be reliable; however, their accuracy and completeness cannot be guaranteed.

Expert Press
www.ExpertPress.net

Table of Contents

Chapter 10

Dedication

I dedicate this book to my family, my parents Earl and Henrine Oliver, who gave me opportunities to succeed in life, my dear friends who encouraged me and believed in me, and my clients who entrust me with their hard-earned wealth.

For My Children

Lastly, I want my children, Hartlei, Stephanie, and Christopher, to know everything I do is all for them.

Introduction

"Retire from work, but not from life."

M.K. Soni

From the time we get our first job waiting tables or bagging groceries, we Americans obsess over retirement. Even folks who love what they do are haunted by thoughts of retirement. It doesn't help that we hear about it all the time.

Despite having a higher median savings account compared to younger generations, Baby Boomers are less confident about their ability to retire than Millennials. Perhaps this is in part because of the way the mainstream media presents retirement for Boomers — as an approaching crisis of little savings and high debt.

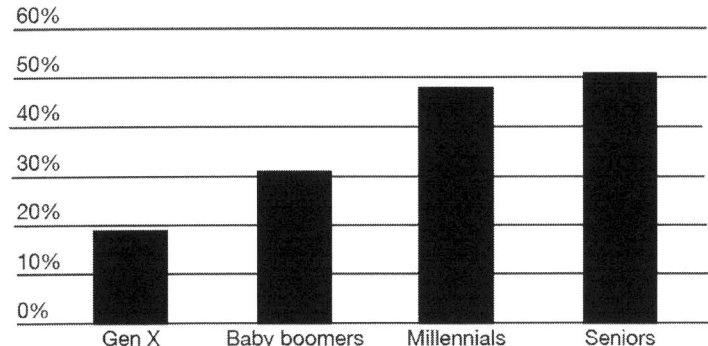

Retirement ready or not?
Percentage of each generation confident they will have enough money to carry themselves post-work

Source: Scottrade's 2016 American Investor Report

The reality, of course, is more complex. There are plenty of people nearing retirement age who would lead happy, fulfilling lives in retirement. But, as a country, when we think of retirement, we envision luxurious cruises, exclusive country club memberships, and a closely guarded horde of funds to bestow upon our loved ones after our death.

Whether or not this vision of retirement is realistic, or even preferable, it is rarely questioned, which leaves most of us with the impression that our choices are an expensive retirement of total leisure or living in poverty and eating cat food.

Spoiler Alert: You are not going to eat cat food in retirement.

I believe this obsession with getting the "right" retirement stems from an innate desire to be successful in our lives. Retirement is not the finish line; it's the victory lap. It shows we've done a good job and are now getting our deserved reward. Retirement is something meaningful.

Or, at least, it should be. Obsessing too much about an unattainable retirement can rob the joy from your retirement years, but not thinking about retirement *enough* can also have devastating consequences.

Without careful consideration and planning, you could very well retire with insufficient funds to live off of and a feeling of financial and mental emptiness. Anxiety, depression, discontent, all of these negative emotions can take root in an unhappy, unplanned retirement.

Retirement income planning has changed drastically over the last three decades. Thirty years ago, most Americans could safely rely on Social Security and a pension to provide the income they needed in retirement. That's no longer the case. Gone are the days of the gold watch and the comfortable pension. Today, we have a much greater personal responsibility to create our own retirement income plan.

In this book, we will look at the critical pieces of your retirement to help give you financial confidence. We'll also look at the emotional and mental aspects of retirement and explore strategies for a happy and fulfilled retirement.

Retirement is more than just a number and a date. Retirement is a lifestyle that is unique to each person. This book will help you navigate retirement planning and devise a plan of action that may offer you less stress and could provide you with guaranteed income for life.

There are some well-known and large areas of finance that we think of when we think of retirement. These include:

* Social Security

* Our existing retirement plans

* Our home

* Personal savings

* Life insurance

* Work insurance

* And pensions

Even if you don't currently have a pension, this book can show you how to create your own pension so that you can possibly have guaranteed money every month.

My hope is that from reading this book, you will walk away with a full understanding of the importance of creating a retirement plan for the success of your future. Moreover, I hope that you will gain a comprehensive knowledge base of retirement planning, what it really means to create a legacy, and the importance of spending your retirement years doing things that enrich your life and bring you joy.

It's incredible what you can do with your life when you are in control of your money, rather than the other way around.

Exercise: Retirement Visualization

Take some time to think about retirement, not only from a financial point of view but a visual one. Write down your definition of a successful retirement.

Chapter 1

The Frustrations of Retirement Planning

"Frustration, although quite painful at times, is a very positive and essential part of success."

Bo Bennett

Consider the everyday stress of modern-day life: traffic, work, marriage, children — not just raising them, but financially providing for them — plus bills, household chores, home repairs. Even your social life can add stress. Now add to that stress ball your 401(k), investments, and of course, the looming aspect of retirement.

Planning for retirement can be very frustrating all on its own, but my hope is that as you read through this book, you will be able to unpack some of the biggest components of retirement so that it doesn't appear as daunting or frustrating.

Whether you're feeling frustration around retirement because you don't know how you'll afford it, or you don't know what you'll do with all that free time — having a plan for your retirement can alleviate the anxiety and negative emotions. And the first step toward creating a plan is understanding the components of retirement planning.

Retirement Is Like Golf
(No, Really)

Oftentimes, I liken retirement planning to the game of golf. Golf can be very frustrating when you have one bad stroke, and then, as the round goes on, you dig yourself deeper into a hole. However, if you relax more and worry less, you're able to focus on one shot at a time, looking for signs of improvement as you play the game and make plans. When you don't take the game quite so seriously, you can enjoy the time spent learning and playing.

Anything worth a measurement of success requires a plan. When iconic basketball player Michael Jordan left college in his junior year to join the NBA and was then drafted by the Chicago Bulls, he had a plan to become one of, if not the best basketball player of his time. He succeeded at that plan because he took the necessary steps to get there and learned from many along the way.

Criticized for his game and the fact that he was a left-hander in a game dominated by right-handers, Phil Mickelson (world-famous golfer) became the first left-hander in 1990 to win the U.S. Amateur title. Yet, he didn't stop there because he had a plan — a plan to achieve even more success in the midst of naysayers. His plan worked, and he won his first PGA Tour tournament as an amateur, shocking his critics.

I remember as a high school student thinking all I needed to do was make $75,000, get married, buy a house, have five children, and then life would be excellent. But I kept asking myself the frustrating question, "How would I be able to accomplish all these successes?" I had no clue. Essentially, I had an idea of my life's success, but I had no plan in place.

I was a teenager; planning isn't typically their strong suit. But, many adults feel this same sense of insecurity when it comes to their retirement.

So, in short, planning helps set direction and priorities in retirement. Sometimes a poor plan is better than no plan at all.

Countdown to Retirement

Although retirement is always on people's minds, many tend to see it as something that is far away from their current reality. They say things like:

- I have plenty of time; I'm only 20 years old.
- I am still in my 30s.
- We just had a baby.
- I am 50, and I can't get caught up.
- I wish I would have.
- I need to earn money fast, so I'm going to take big financial risks and hope they pay off.

Truthfully, we are always counting down to retirement. In your 20s, you're not thinking about it because, in your mind, you have forever. Then all of a sudden, you hit your 30s, and you start to build a family and your responsibilities increase, so you put off retirement until later. Suddenly, your small family grows from one child to two or more. The next thing you know, you're just getting yourself back together while you've stepped into your fifties.

This is the essence of the countdown. It's the classic wisdom from the older generation to the younger: *It all goes by so fast.* It's true, but if you're one of the many people who didn't start planning for retirement until later in life, don't panic. Starting your retirement plan in your 40s or 50s doesn't mean you've missed the boat. It means you have an opportunity to start today. Even if you're 50 years old, this is probably a good time to make some necessary changes so you do have a successful retirement.

Think of it like being on a yo-yo diet. When you put off planning for retirement, it's as if you lost weight through a fad diet, then binged on cookie-dough ice cream for a week. We give ourselves permission with thoughts like, "As long as I only gain five pounds," or "As long as I can still wear these jeans." With the retirement countdown, we make excuses by saying that next year we'll start planning our retirement, and when next year comes, we put it off again. And again, and again. *I'll start as soon as I hit 45; I'll start as soon as I pay off something.*

You'll never find a good time to start, but the best time to start is right now.

You may be wondering *what* exactly you should start. We'll get there. I'm going to walk you through all the steps of building a retirement plan that gives you the financial awareness and personal confidence you need to live happily and productively.

The Formula for Retirement Planning

What if you're 50 years old right now and have no idea where you should start planning your retirement? Well, you start by connecting with a retirement investment planner. When I meet with clients for retirement planning, I always find out if they have a retirement opportunity or retirement benefits through their place of employment. People are more likely to put away for retirement if they use a company plan where the money is automatically taken out of their paychecks.

If they don't, then there are other ways they can put away money, like in an individual retirement account (IRA). The first priority is determining what retirement savings options are available. Retirement accounts like 401(k)s and IRAs have tax benefits and are a good place to start.

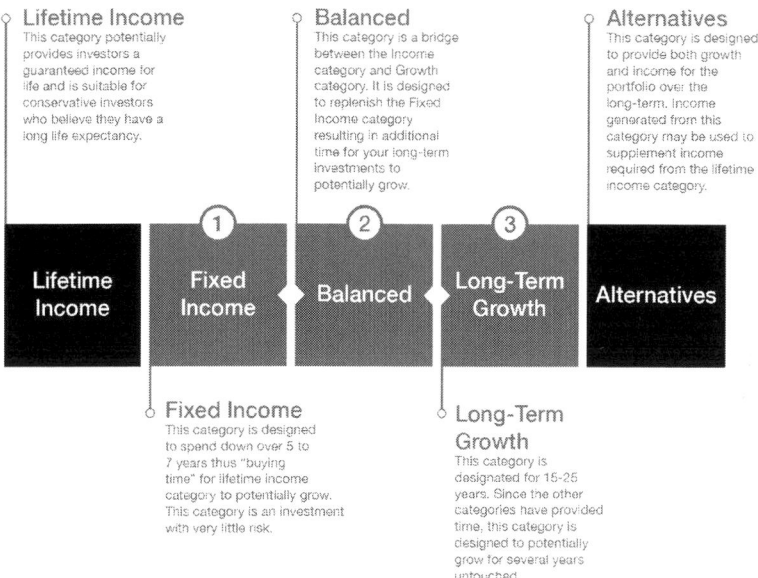

Lifetime Income
This category potentially provides investors a guaranteed income for life and is suitable for conservative investors who believe they have a long life expectancy.

Balanced
This category is a bridge between the Income category and Growth category. It is designed to replenish the Fixed Income category resulting in additional time for your long-term investments to potentially grow.

Alternatives
This category is designed to provide both growth and income for the portfolio over the long-term. Income generated from this category may be used to supplement income required from the lifetime income category.

| Lifetime Income | ① Fixed Income | ② Balanced | ③ Long-Term Growth | Alternatives |

Fixed Income
This category is designed to spend down over 5 to 7 years thus "buying time" for lifetime income category to potentially grow. This category is an investment with very little risk.

Long-Term Growth
This category is designated for 15-25 years. Since the other categories have provided time, this category is designed to potentially grow for several years untouched.

The second priority is finding a comfortable amount of money you can start putting away on a weekly or bi-weekly basis, taken directly out of your bank account. If you have a company plan option, the contribution may be deducted straight from your paycheck. If you do not have a retirement account through work, your contribution should be automatically deducted from your bank account. Obviously, if you're in debt, and a lot of debt, that's something you need to consider. Give yourself a financial checkup before you start saving for retirement.

- Are you making enough to pay all your bills?
- If not, what bills or expenses can be adjusted?
- If all the bills are paid, how much is left?

- How much could you put in the retirement account? How much do you want to keep in your savings account?

If you have a large but manageable amount of debt, you may try a hybrid approach of paying down debt while also putting away a little bit for retirement. The goal is to have minimal debt and a sizable retirement nest egg by the time you retire. Also, human nature tells us that if you do not take action, nothing will change.

The vision for retirement may not be clear from your 20s. Likewise, the vision can be frightening from your 50s and create a sense of helplessness. No matter where you are in the retirement spectrum, starting today will help you. There is a difference between HOPE, DREAMS, and a PLAN. This book will provide actionable topics that, if taken seriously, can greatly improve your ability to achieve a unique, successful retirement and possibly increase your chances for financial security.

You have to start now because time is on your side. Even if you're 50, 30, or 25 years old, you can make a huge difference.

Visualizing Your Retirement

So when you think about visualizing your retirement, sit down and give some deep thought as to what you want to do and what is going to make your retirement successful.

If, in retirement, you want to golf every day, travel the world, go out to dinner every night, and spoil the grandkids — that's great.

Now ask yourself: Who's going to pay for all of it?

If you haven't saved a lot of money, you're not going to be able to do most of those things. In many cases, I work with clients to formulate more realistic goals of what they would like to do.

There are plenty of people who want to retire just so they have the freedom to do things that they always wanted to try. That may be as simple as setting up a separate business, knowing that they have enough money to fall back on. There are others who want to begin hobbies and volunteer with charities. It could even be as simple as downsizing their home or moving somewhere that they never would have taken the chance to move to before they retired.

Some people say they'd like to spend a lot of time with their grandchildren or do some hobbies and travel. Some of my clients want to take the first five years of retirement and travel as a big family to exotic places. Brainstorm your bucket list and include anything and everything that is important to you. Want to mentor? Put it down. Always dreamed of learning to paint? On the list. That novel you never finished in college? Now's your time to shine.

Once you have your list, you must determine what is realistic and what's most important. All right? Can you do all of these things? Which are most important to you, and which are most realistic? It doesn't mean you're crossing any of them off as impossible. You're just prioritizing the ones that are more realistic and will give you the most fulfillment.

We also talk about some fears in retirement. I find with my clients that their biggest fears are:

* Running out of money
* Getting scammed in their old age
* Out-of-pocket healthcare costs

All of these are things you cannot control.

That may sound scary, but here's some good news: None of these should keep you from achieving your visualized retirement. If a client is worried about healthcare expenses, I might counsel them to take one big family vacation the first year of retirement and then keep a small nest egg just in case they need it later. It's important when planning your retirement to talk about contingency plans, the backups and fail-safes that will help you from running out of money or living a meager, unfulfilling retirement. Long-term care coverage is one of those fail-safes. There's a high probability that either you or your spouse, or possibly both, will need long-term care at some point in your lives.

A map is always helpful to reach a new destination. Visualizing your retirement helps you draw a map of how you'll get there. Some folks may get lucky enough to fall into an unplanned and totally happy retirement, but for most, lack of planning comes back to bite them at some point. It's interesting that we all talk about retirement ad nauseam, but no one actually sits down and puts pen to paper. But we know that when there's a written realistic goal, people have a road map and can make decisions that move them toward the goal. They're able to think long term. Maybe you don't need to purchase that slick new sports car. Maybe you don't even need a new car at all. Would the money be better spent on a week in the mountains with family? Or a second honeymoon cruise with your spouse? Or socked away in case of a healthcare incident? You don't know until you sit down and plan. Retirement planning is equal parts aspiration and pragmatism.

Then, there are other scenarios that one may face in retirement planning. What if you have an investment that goes bad? What do you do? This type of anxious thinking can quickly derail your plans to save and invest for retirement or to spend the money you've earned after you've stopped working. Don't let this happen to you. The trick is to remember this is a long game. You have to visualize the entire journey, not just tomorrow.

When a golfer steps up to take a shot, they visualize where the ball will land. They're "seeing" the actions they need to take to impact the ball's trajectory in a positive way that positions it in or near the hole. Retirement isn't that much different. You're looking down at your life from afar; you're talking to yourself about what you're trying to achieve, and you must believe that it can happen. You know, obviously, the most important thing is execution in any sport.

Executing in retirement planning is having discipline and sticking to the script or, basically, the blueprint that has been written. Obviously, a real-life situation may cause you to pivot momentarily, but the goal is to get back on track toward that vision as quickly as possible. We pivot; we don't panic. We don't stop investing because the stock market had one bad day. We don't liquidate all of our accounts because we need minor surgery. What do you do? The same thing a golfer does when they accidentally land in a sand trap: You get the ball back in the fairway, and you keep playing to win.

Life happens. Don't let it derail you. If you forget that last shot, you keep going. That's important to the plan, and you can't let one bad shot ruin your entire round.

Look forward, not backward; don't dwell on what happened in the past. If you look in reverse, you're not going to go forward. You're going to go in the direction you're looking. That's one reason not to look at the stock market every day. You should monitor it, but you don't need to be looking at it all the time.

The same is true for your retirement. You have to "see" where you are going in order to get there.

> There is perhaps nothing more critical in a relationship than communication, especially around finances. Now is the time to discuss your retirement vision with your spouse so that you're on the same page.

Growing up, my father worked for General Electric as an engineer. He'd planned to retire at 55 and start a real estate business. Unfortunately, he either never had a chance or never took the time to explain that plan to my mother. My mother thought he was going to retire and that the two of them were just going to work on some of the things that needed to be fixed around the house and then spend more time playing golf and doing things together.

He was interested in starting a side business, and that created a lot of friction because he never told her the plan. I think, frankly, if they would have had a discussion earlier about their retirement expectations, things would've been a little more smooth.

I think it's important to have that discussion and, in order to have a meaningful conversation about expectations, you first have to have the vision. Encourage your spouse to envision *their* retirement vision, too. Then you can both come to the table and see if your visions and expectations are aligned. That discussion should occur, first and foremost, before you even think about retiring.

Pieces in Your Retirement Puzzle

So, when does the retirement plan begin? Is it something that you should put together in your 20s and 30s?

Actually, one common thing with our successful retirees and pre-retirees is that they all start saving early — and they save often. As soon as you start the workforce and have access to a company retirement plan, take advantage of it. It's all about the power of compound interest. The faster you start, the better off you'll be. Essentially, you will have a longer time for those investments to grow. Folks have other life priorities to think about and save for when they're in their twenties — student loans, marriage, homeownership, children, etc. But, if you can start a retirement account in your twenties, you're ahead of the game.

Retirement Savings Tips for Young Families

And there are things that people can do in their 20s that actually will build their retirement plan and can also provide protection for their future.

You might be able to put together an insurance policy. Your young family may not have lots of money to put away, but you may be able to structure something that has a compound growth — not just in terms of growing the money but by accomplishing two or three goals simultaneously because you understand how it all works. In short, there are investments that can provide protection for your family and retirement income.

The number one goal is protecting the family, and insurance plays a very big part of it. Believe it or not, there are insurance products where you can accumulate cash for retirement while also providing protection for your family.

I advise most of our younger clients that, if their employer offers a retirement savings plan and offers a match minimally, they should try to put away as much as they're offering for the match. Think of it as free money that would be all yours.

So, if you put 5 percent in an employer-matched retirement account, they match your 5 percent deposit to your 401(k). You get 10 percent for the cost of 5 percent.

Now, in order for you to put in that matching 5 percent contribution, it may mean that you have to pull the belt a little tighter. However, over 30 years of this contribution will turn into a fairly nice retirement plan.

The Retirement "Box Top"

At my firm, we use our own segmentation to provide you with some financial confidence when investing. We have seen this process work over time, as it allows our retirees to make better decisions instead of making knee-jerk reactions to the stock market. Knee-jerk reactions and emotions with investor assets cause poor decisions and less than desirable returns.

Buying high and selling low is never a good strategy for long-term investors and retirees. In a scenario like this, the investor anxiously watches the market every day, getting minute-by-minute updates. When the market drops 30 percent, they sell everything. And now they're toast. Was that necessarily the best plan? Perhaps not!

In reality, most of the time, the market is going to come right back up. We've seen it happen time and time again.

Segmentation also manages your risk. Basically, segmentation is dividing assets into three categories. We want a **Today Bucket**, which are assets that you're going to need to live off of. We're going to look at the **Tomorrow Bucket** for down the road. And then we're going to look for a **Later Bucket** for the distant future.

In other words, you're segmenting your money to better safe-guard against the mistakes that people make all the time. You will take very little risk in your Today Bucket because you are living off of it and can't afford to take that risk.

We segment the money because there are blips in the market and unexpected expenses happen, and we want to know that there's "Tomorrow Bucket" money down the road. And we don't have to worry about it.

Let's look at two theoretical clients: couple Jones and couple Roberts. The Jones' are financially comfortable and like to take more risks with their money. They would put more money in their Later Bucket. Remember, the Later Bucket is your legacy money down the road. Since they have a 25-year plan for retirement, it doesn't matter if the market goes up, down, or sideways. They have a long horizon.

For the more risk-averse Roberts', they will work more in the Tomorrow Bucket, where they will get lower returns and experience less risk. The Roberts want liquidity, but most importantly, they want to feel more confident in their returns.

Okay, so we've discussed today's money, tomorrow's money, and someday's money. This book will act as your guide. If you were to put together a puzzle, it's helpful to have the box top showing the picture. Consider this book your box top. I'm going to help you find all of your pieces, sort them out, and then put them together.

Your box top is your guide to putting the retirement plan puzzle pieces together:

Corner Pieces 1st – Today's Money

Edge Pieces 2nd – Tomorrow's Money

Center Pieces 3rd – Legacy Money

The process in this book will help you segment your retirement dollars in a way that is unique to your personal retirement wishes, both financially and emotionally. It is designed to help reduce your worry during a complex time in your financial life.

The First Retirement Conversation

The first thing I do when meeting a new client is to talk to them about the three F's: **family, finances, and feelings.**

Family. How is your family doing? Will an in-law or other family members be living with you during your retirement? Is there any illness in your family? Is there anything we should know about your family that could derail or cause a little bit of pressure on your retirement?

Finances. How healthy are your finances? Do you have a savings account, 401(k), pension, investments? Do you have any debt?

Have you lost money, are you expecting money, or is there a windfall of money on its way?

Feelings. Most important, we talk about feelings, which is really a conversation about risk. How risk averse are you? You need to be brutally honest in the initial planning process. On the investment side, we just want to make sure that we are solving for income, inflation, and risk. And we'll do that in a sense that's unique to your current situation.

Discussing Retirement Realities

Imagine having your life savings for retirement, and you are enjoying your life. Everything is fine. You have money to live on, the house is paid off, and you are enjoying the comfortable lifestyle you proposed on your whiteboard. One day life throws you a curve and you need assisted living and care. How will you pay for it? Will you self-insure? Do you qualify for aid? It may sound scary or too doom and gloom, but believe me — it's better to face your retirement planning with your eyes open and all the facts in front of you. Did you know that you must deplete all your assets before the government considers you eligible for aid? What about the legacy? What about the kids and grandkids? Why not make a financial plan complete by addressing a probable need. A sound retirement plan provides for some sort of long-term care while preserving the corpus of your wealth that you desire to pass on to the next generation.

[Exercise:]

How do I know which assets to liquidate in retirement?

There are a series of circumstances to determine which assets to liquidate in retirement.

① Identify untouchable assets. These are assets that have been handed down from generation to generation.

② Think about taxation. Some assets, like collectibles, could be taxed at 28 percent or more.

③ Keep cash on hand. Continue to keep an emergency fund of three to six months of spending, depending on your income sources.

Chapter 2

Retirement Is a Long Game

**"The quality, not the longevity,
of one's life is what is important."**

Martin Luther King, Jr.

Longevity: The Retirement Problem

My attempt is not to try and be cunning in giving this section the title it has. Maybe you would not have considered placing these two words together: retirement and problem. However, there is an unavoidable issue or problem we all face with retirement — longevity.

Will we outlive our money?

Essentially, people are living longer than they anticipated and longer than the financial market anticipated as well. If you plan on living into your 90s or 100s (and honestly, who doesn't?), you need to plan for your retirement money to live with you.

Longevity is a good thing; it's great that preventive wellness measures and modern medicine breakthroughs allow us all to live healthier for longer. But, when it comes to retirement, longevity is a risk multiplier. Years ago, people didn't worry about retirement as much, because quite frankly, they didn't live as long.

Average U.S. Life Expectancy from 1950 to 2020

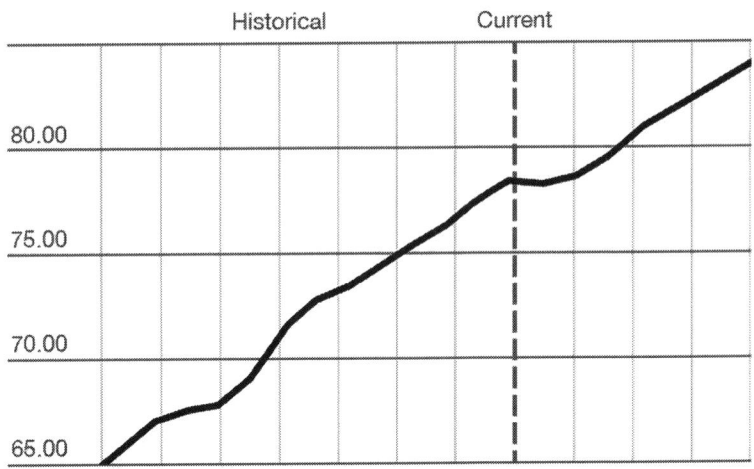

Data Source: U.N. World Population Prospects

Centenarians are becoming more common every day. There's even a category now called the supercentenarians, who are the people that live past 110! Years ago, that was barely ever heard of, but quite frankly, it's happening all the time.

Now that living to 100 is a more common occurrence, it's important to plan a retirement budget that takes longevity into account. If you only plan on living to 85, and you spend your retirement finances like you're only living to 85, but then you live to be 100 … you're at a much greater risk for finding yourself short on cash in those later years. Retirement is about planning for the long game. You need a retirement plan that matches your longevity.

Whatever Happened to Willard Scott?

Does anyone remember Willard Scott? Willard Scott used to be an anchor on TV for the "Today" show. Twice a week, he would spend 25 minutes announcing the birthday of someone who turned 100 years old. It was quite an event for everyone to watch on television. Eventually, they stopped making these announcements because there were too many people to announce.

When I meet with new clients, I like to ask them about their parents, and when they tell me their mother lived to be 95 or both of their parents are still alive, which is very common, I carefully process what I'm hearing. Longevity is fantastic, but it's something you have to plan for.

Population of the U.S. by Year of Age in 2015

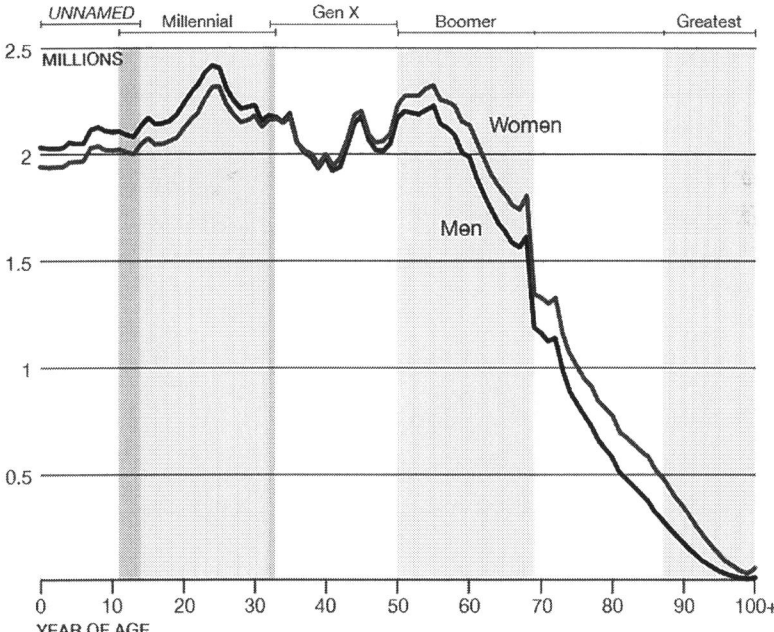

Source: Census Bureau. Generational boundaries from Pew Research, demographers.

I also ask about their health. This may seem morbid, but the reality is more clients appreciate the honest and frank discussion of their expected lifetimes after retirement. They know they need a plan, and to make one, we first need to lay out the facts.

If you're in relatively good health and long lifespans run in your family, you should plan to live between 95 and 100 at least, just to be safe.

The Baby Boomer generation is interesting. They have more medical advancements available to them, but they've also lived more of their lives at desk jobs, exercising less often, and eating more fast food.

It's always best to plan on the side of longevity. You can always bequeath your excess funds in your will, but you can't go back in time and spend less at the beginning of your retirement. Not planning for the long game can lead to a real retirement crisis: outliving your money.

No One is Eating Cat Food

Let's be clear: When I'm talking about running out of money, I'm not talking about the dreaded "eating cat food to survive" stereotype. Cat food is more expensive than a bowl of Maruchan Ramen, so why this stereotype continues to exist baffles me. The point is that when we say, "running out of money," we typically mean that clients are worried that they will no longer be able to afford their lifestyle. For affluent retirees, this may mean downsizing their homes or forgoing expensive vacations, but more modest retirees may have to face tougher choices. I can certainly understand the concern of this kind. With that being said, being a burden on the family is another concern.

Pension-izing Your Retirement

Years ago, most people had pensions. Remember the retiree stereotype: a silver-haired man lying in a hammock having a glass of iced tea and reading the paper because 70-75 percent of his income is covered by his pension, and the rest is covered by Social Security and a little bit of savings? Sounds like a dream, right? It is. The dream of retirement. And that's what we all want.

That dream is possible, even though pensions are largely a thing of the past.

By reading the rest of this book and following the plan laid out in its pages, you can actually achieve a dream retirement of sustainable income for life. Whatever plan we come up with for you is going to be unique to you and not what society tells you.

The goal is to create a pension-like payment plan with your current retirement assets like your IRA, 401(k), and other retirement accounts. That means determining a fixed amount of "income" you can draw from these assets for your retirement expenses.

A pension is basically a definitive and guaranteed benefit plan given by employers to employees in the form of a fixed payout at retirement.

When I think about the clients I see at our practice, the happiest seem to be the government workers, teachers, and police officers. Why are police officers, government workers, and teachers so happy in retirement? Pensions, pensions, pensions!

I believe the happiest people during retirement are those with some sort of guaranteed income because it removes at least one anxiety from their retirement plan. Wouldn't it be nice to know that no matter what, your basic living expenses will be covered? So, if the stock market or real estate market goes up, down, or sideways, are your paychecks waiting for you in your bank account? When you lock in the rent money, it helps create a budget but also takes away the fear of outliving your money. Guaranteed income gives you confidence that your checks will be there every single month for as long as you're there to open the envelope.

Today, most employers no longer offer pensions.

So, how does someone get guaranteed income that can be relied upon? The best way is to determine how much money your money makes and consider that your guaranteed income.

If you have $500,000 in a retirement fund with a roughly 5 percent return, then you can safely spend $25,000 without ever dipping into your actual retirement fund. Now add in your Social Security benefit. For this example, we will use the national average benefit of just over $17,500. We now have $42,500 in "guaranteed" income.

It's not quite that simple, but there are products and planning that can help achieve "guaranteed income." That's not "rich" retirement money, but it certainly is livable, especially if you have a fixed expense budget.

We find that if you have the fixed expenses of your life taken care of now, the other critical part is obviously working on your health. The question we ask our clients is: "How do you want to retire?" This is a valid and important question. Retirement is not a one-way ticket to the grave; therefore, you still want to live an abundant life to the fullest for as long as you can.

Understanding Social Security

A golfer has many clubs to choose from; however, they have to understand how each one is different and how best to utilize it to achieve the objective. What's the difference between a 3-iron and a 7-iron? A pitching wedge and a sand wedge?

Can't I just use whichever one I want? Well, yes and no. Yes, you certainly can. But no, not if you want to score a birdie or eagle on the green.

A bag full of strangely named clubs may be overwhelming and complex, especially if you don't understand it. The same can be said of Social Security. It's got a lot of useful filing strategies, but it can absolutely overwhelm newcomers. And almost all retirees are newcomers when it comes time to filing for Social Security.

When preparing retirement cases for our clients, we want to take steps to make sure that there is money for the rest of their lives, and that can come in two different ways. Advisors were telling clients in their sixties to take the necessary steps to maximize their Social Security benefit, as many of you may already know. Social Security is more complex than many realize. It is also a lifeline for millions of Americans. There are about 500 ways to claim Social Security, and how you file affects your benefit check. It's sort of like your taxes; it pays to have an expert help you correctly file so you get the most amount of money possible, which is, remember, the amount that you deserve. A married couple could be looking at a million-dollar benefit. Unfortunately, most people take a reduced benefit because they do not know the consequences.

Social Security Filing Tips

Wait if You Can

The longer you defer taking your Social Security benefit, the bigger the eventual check will be. For more on this, see "When to Start Receiving Social Security Benefits."

Working

You can continue to work after you start receiving Social Security benefits. However, if you are under full retirement age and earn over a certain threshold, some of your benefit will be withheld. You will receive a larger benefit when you reach full retirement age. Working part time during the early years of your retirement, if you retire before full retirement age, can actually increase the value of your total lifetime benefit.

Widows

In general, a person who is widowed should claim the survivor benefit as soon they can do so and allow their own benefit to continue to grow. If, however, the deceased partner already had a substantially larger benefit, the widow should file for their own benefit first, then switch to the deceased partner's benefit later.

Plan With an Expert

Social Security is a lifetime benefit, and with the proper planning between husband and wife, it could be a benefit worth as much as a million dollars. That kind of money means filing for Social Security is serious business. So, take it seriously. Meet with an advisor. Find out how you should file to get the benefits you deserve.

When to Start Receiving Social Security Benefits

Taking Social Security payments too early means receiving less money each month than you would receive if you waited for even a few years. If possible, do not begin taking Social Security until you are at least your full retirement age. If you take Social Security benefits at age 62, your benefit will be approximately 25 to 30 percent less than if you had waited until your full retirement age. Full retirement is a sliding scale from 65-67, depending on the date of birth, so you should check with an advisor on what "full retirement" means for you.

For an even bigger benefit, wait until age 70, when your payment will be at least 75 percent higher than if you started taking benefits at 62.

By working longer, you can delay taking Social Security benefits, and you may also be able to increase the size of your Social Security benefit based on additional years of earnings and/ or higher wages. You'll add to your nest egg and prolong any healthcare coverage you may have. Also, your spouse will receive your benefit if you are the higher wage earner.

Plan for Longevity ... and the Unexpected

Your retirement plan should be created especially for you, not what somebody else says you should be doing in retirement. It should show how much money you'll be able to depend on for the duration of your life, even if you live to be 125. It should also have details and contingency plans in case something happens to you early in retirement.

For example, say a father dies suddenly in a motorcycle accident. He has already established a retirement plan, proper insurance, and everything. Fortunately, he also ended up with a pension from the fire department. Is that part of a retirement plan? Where does that fit into the picture?

A will or trust gives you the ability to direct your financial wishes to where you want them to go. Having your will or trust up to date is absolutely imperative. It even plays a part in terms of difficult healthcare decisions.

If you suffer a catastrophic health event, like an aneurysm or a stroke (and God forbid such a thing should happen, but we know from data that they do all the time), and you are left in a vegetative state, what should your family do? With a medical directive, your wishes are known. In fact, in some states, patients cannot be removed from life support without a medical directive.

Another unexpected situation is the jealous animosity that crops up after a loved one's death. You don't want your family members fighting over their share of the inheritance. You also don't want a judge or the court to decide where your lifelong savings end up. It should be up to us to make that decision. Then give that information to a competent trust and estate attorney. At the bare minimum, you should have a will and all beneficiary designation forms.

Why You Need a Will

When a wealthy client sits down with me to talk about retirement, we're usually talking about dollars and cents. What they're not considering is how the millions of dollars they've saved to give as an inheritance could be lost if their estate goes into probate. This is another reason why it's so important to have a plan that your spouse is aligned with and your children are aware of. You don't want your hard-earned money to go to waste, and you don't want your family arguing over their share of the inheritance after you're gone. A well-constructed will can prevent both of these things.

Your will should include, at a minimum, the following things:

- A list of all financial assets
- Real property, such as your home
- Beneficiaries
- A clear designation of assets and property to beneficiaries

Mentally Prepare for Retirement

The number one objective for most if not all people is to retire with dignity. The first step toward that goal is a solid retirement financial plan and retirement strategy. The second step is a little tougher: You've got to create a positive retirement outlook.

How do you do that? It starts with your retirement vision. What do you want retirement to look like? Lots of golf, fishing, travel? Mentorship and active participation with your church? More time with the grandkids? Whatever it is, write it down in the form of a plan and a vision.

Now that you have a vision, you need actionable, achievable goals to help you get there. What do you need to do in order to live the retirement you've envisioned? What changes to your lifestyle will you need to make now? Five years from now? When you retire? Don't try to make all the changes at once. Change is hard, and too much at once can be overwhelming. If you need to save more, start by setting a goal to reduce your miscellaneous spending. Good? Good! Now, how much more could you put toward your debt? Make one small positive change at a time.

The Secret Downside of Retirement

Anxiety, depression, guilt. These are not emotions many associate with retirement, but I assure you they are more common than you might think. It's important to be honest with yourself before you retire. Retirement is, in some ways, like becoming a parent. It is a huge lifestyle change, and even if you look forward to it, the reality may leave you feeling a little ambivalent.

If you are a Type A person who has worked your whole life, putting food on the table, or running powerful board meetings, you should consider that retirement may leave you feeling bored or without purpose.

Some retirees look at everything they have and feel a sense of guilt: *I have so much and so many have so little.* This guilt can be paralyzing, but it can also motivate a fulfilling and awesome life of philanthropy and civic work in your retired years. The trick is to be able to identify what you are feeling and why.

Finally, if you are facing retirement with far less than you had hoped for, you may feel depressed. Depression is an illness — it can impact your overall health and damage relationships you treasure.

For all of these, the advice I give is to talk about it. Talk to your spouse or partner, your clergyman or rabbi, your best friend, and possibly a professional. Being proactive about your mental health before retirement is one powerful and important step toward achieving the retirement you're dreaming of.

When Retirement Means Downsizing

I would love it if all my clients retired with piles of cash in their accounts, but that isn't the reality for many Americans. If retirement for you is going to involve life changes like downsizing your home or changing your spending habits, it's important to work on a mental shift that allows you to feel happy and fulfilled through the changes.

Many do not consider this side of it, but retirement is also a mental process. Changing your normal routine that you have been used to for years is not a small feat. Even folks with no financial worries often feel a post-retirement depression as they adjust to life without work. What the retirement life shift does to someone's psyche and how it makes them feel about themselves is significant. That plays into what kind of retirement and later years they're going to have.

One way to accept a downsize in your life is confidence in your future, and that's what a guaranteed income for life brings.

If your Social Security, pension, annuities, and other finances can sustain a moderate lifestyle throughout your retired life, you won't have to worry about money and can focus on doing things that make you *happy*.

*Having Guaranteed Income for Life = Financial Co*nfidence

What Makes You Happy?

Remember that old song by Bobby McFerrin, "Don't Worry Be Happy"? Well, it's true. There are many things people can worry about, especially when it comes to retirement. And worrying steals your joy; it's difficult to be happy when you're only worrying. McFerrin defined happiness as singing and dancing to the music of life. So, how do you define happiness? It's different for everybody.

Happiness for me is going on a beach vacation, the first cup of coffee in the morning, or reading the paper on the porch like my family did, which I couldn't stand as a kid. These are the things that make me happy.

Remember in "The Sound of Music" when Maria Rainer encouraged the von Trapp children to list a few of their favorite things to cheer them up? This is what you should do to prepare for retirement.

Note: Income, assets, or returns do not define happiness. Travel, reading, time with family, cooking for loved ones, learning new things, golfing, relaxing in the sun — those may just be a few of your favorite things.

Retirement happiness is a combination of financial confidence and achieving the goals, aspirations, and desires you've chosen as important. Everyone's happiness is defined at different stages in life, but also unique to you.

Exercise:

What changes will you make for your retirement? What can you sacrifice, and what do you refuse to give up?

Chapter 3

Successful Habits of Retirees

"As in all successful ventures, the foundation of a good retirement is planning."

Earl Nightingale

According to Business Insider, there are 13 major habits of successful millionaires. For the purposes of this book, I'll focus on the top five:

- They read consistently.
- They spend time with other successful people.
- They have multiple sources of income.
- They help others succeed.
- They seek feedback.

You'll notice that the common thread of these successful habits is action — putting their plan to succeed into action. Oftentimes, we find that it's easy to talk about something in the abstract but harder to put pen to paper and maintain the discipline to plan for the future. That isn't restricted to planning for retirement. People talk about losing weight, going back to school, or writing a book, but for a lot of them, it never goes farther than talk. Discipline, though, is made up of practicing a few simple habits until they become part of your routine.

Trying to lose weight? Your first habit might be to walk 10,000 steps every day. Another might be to stop eating desserts or late-night snacks. If you want to write a book, the first habit is to write something — anything — every day.

Remember, success comes after a plan has been set. So, taking the time to map out a plan and sticking to that plan is paramount.

I mentioned in an earlier chapter that as a kid, I thought all I needed to be successful was to make $75,000 a year, have five children, a house, and a dog. Quite frankly, that was just a wish list and a dream. I thought that a life like this would solve all of life's problems. Yet, I had no plan on how to do it. Welcome to the real world. You actually have to plan for the real world and pay for everything that you're wishing for.

Dedication, commitment, discipline — these are what separate plans from wish lists. You can't just wish for a confident, fulfilling retirement. You've got to invest in it.

Another Golf Analogy

Retirement planning is kind of like golf. I'm pretty passionate about golf; as you can tell from my previous examples, I play all the time. When the weather's nice I try to golf twice a week. I have been doing this for the last 15 years. Golf provides me an opportunity to spend quality time with clients, family, and friends while enjoying the fresh air, getting some exercise, and having some fun. How is all that like retirement planning? Because golf requires commitment and practice. When I first started playing golf, I wasn't as good as I am now. It took years of regular practice. I could have gotten frustrated that I wasn't Tiger Woods from my first swing, but I didn't. I stuck with it, and I enjoyed every game I played.

I can't tell you how many times I've seen people get to the first couple of holes and say they want to quit because they're not getting the results they expected fast enough, or they find it frustrating. Again, the same thing happens with our retirement plans. You won't see the immediate gratification in the beginning, but if you take it on a segmented hole-by-hole approach, in the end, 10-20 years later, you will see the success. This is the advantage of mapping out a realistic plan.

Small Drips Make a Big Puddle

For nongolfers, think of retirement saving like a New Year's resolution. It's popular for everyone to make a declaration about their new life choices or to set up their goals with the greatest of intentions. Some of these may include getting out of debt, quitting smoking, or losing weight. After not seeing any real results after a couple of weeks, they go back to their old habits: eating unhealthy foods, buying a pack a day, or spending more than they earn. This is the same thing that happens with retirement planning.

When you don't have a solid plan for retirement, saving can become very abstract. It's hard to see how saving a small amount each month will pay off in the long run. When people don't understand the plan for retirement or don't believe in it, they give up easily. The truth is even just $50 a month helps feed your retirement savings. A small but steady drip can make a big puddle over time.

As long as you create a realistic plan and stick to it, you'll find a lot more success. When I say realistic, I mean that your goals have to be attainable. For example, you're certainly not going to lose 100 pounds in a month. You certainly won't save several hundred thousand dollars in a year. And unless you're a VERY good golfer, you're not going to shoot par on your first round.

Having realistic expectations is important. Setting expectations allows you greater discipline because you're less likely to get discouraged or frustrated when you don't see results right away. Saving $50 or $100 a month is practice for the game of retirement. Putting good habits like these into everyday practice will not only get you through the game but help you win it.

Retirement planning must become an actionable habit of putting aside a certain amount of money every month. This small step toward proactively managing your investment will reduce the frustrations of retirement planning.

Create a Retirement Bucket List

We all have a little bit of regret about some things we should've done. I've heard many people say that they're waiting for the day they can take a dream trip, make an investment, or own something. Then that day never comes. I once had a client who dreamed of owning a beach house. He waited and waited and waited, and finally, he felt ready to make the purchase. Six months later, he passed away. His lifelong dream was to have this beach house and enjoy it with his family. His family still has that beach house, but he was never able to enjoy it with them. I say that if you have things on your bucket list, achieve them in your earlier parts of retirement, your "go-go" years. Realistically, you're not going to achieve some of those goals when you hit your "slow-go years," the upper 80s and 90s. Certainly, you're not going to enjoy it as much as you would today. I think bucket lists are healthy and satisfying.

It may sound morbid to list things you want to do before you "kick the bucket," but actually, a bucket list can be a very positive and affirming part of your retirement. Your bucket list can include financial goals you wish to achieve before retirement: eliminate debt, pay off the mortgage, etc. Your bucket list should also include aspirational things you'd like to accomplish during retirement. Some of the most common are:

- Travel more
- Spend more time with family
- Go back to school
- Start a small business
- Mentor or volunteer
- Be more involved with my place of worship
- Write my memoirs

Whatever is on your bucket list, it's important to have one. Successful retirees make sure they live life to the fullest and achieve the goals they have waited so long to achieve.

Once you've written down your bucket list, compare it with your retirement financial plan. Is your bucket list realistic given the budget you will have when you stop working? If you haven't saved for a vineyard, you're not going to own a vineyard someday.

Your bucket list should take your health into account as well. If you want to climb a mountain or complete a triathlon, you'll need to be in pretty good shape. Is getting in shape one of your pre-retirement goals? Do you have a plan that will help you commit to your fitness regime?

You may want to schedule out your bucket list so that more of the physically demanding goals fall in the "go-go" years of retirement. Later in life, it will be a little more difficult to achieve some of those goals just because of age.

Whatever is on your bucket list, make sure you're staying healthy and have allocated the time and resources to do these things.

Bucket lists are great for pre-retirees and retirees alike. If you have another 20 years before you retire, your bucket list should include items like eliminating debt, paying off the house, and putting additional income into your retirement plan. You may not be able to do them *right now*, but having them on a written bucket list reminds you of their importance. If you know you want to take fascinating excursions all over the world during your retirement, then your pre-retirement bucket list should include setting up a retirement plan that will afford you those vacations.

A pre-retirement bucket list makes retirement less intangible. That $50 a month you're squirreling away isn't just "for retirement." It's for the houseboat you and your partner want so you can explore the United States by rivers, lakes, and sea. Good for you! When you have an aspirational goal in mind, it makes the sacrifice easier.

Find Your Purpose

One emotion that many retirees feel and that surprises many pre-retirees is *ennui*. That vague sense of listlessness and aimlessness may surprise those of you who are counting the days until you can golf, travel, and nap as much as you want, but if you are a career-minded, goal-driven person, a life of leisure might only *sound* great. If you have been working all your life to provide for your family or achieve high levels of success in your field, retirement can leave you feeling empty. It's not uncommon for new retirees to feel like they've lost their identity. I hear retirees talk about when they were at a particular company or when they taught at the university, reflecting on their occupation. I try to gently warn them of the difficulty in walking away from the life and schedule that they've always known. You've dedicated years of service doing something, and it's been taken away, and all you're doing now is reflecting on the memories.

This is why smart retirees find purpose outside of work before they retire. If business is your business, you may enjoy a mentorship program. Or, if you have an entrepreneurial spirit, you may want to start a small business. But your purpose doesn't have to be work related. It could be acting as a positive role model to your grandchildren, volunteering with a cause that matters to you, or going back to school. I once met a retiree who began a part-time job driving a few hours a week, a few days a week. And he does it about six months out of the year because he plays golf or other leisure activities the rest of the year. Driving keeps him active and engaging with the customers. Whatever it is, it should fill you with joy and fulfillment.

The other important part of finding your purpose is having a schedule. Routine helps establish normalcy in a new and unfamiliar situation — retirement. Think about retirement and what that will mean to you; it is a complete change in your everyday habit of getting up, possibly commuting, and working in a structure. Having an active schedule that keeps you going to bed and waking up as usual can help you ease into retirement living.

One smart tip I share with clients is to do a practice retirement to see how it feels. Take a sabbatical if you can, or as you approach retirement, shift from full time to part time. I have seen retirees who look like they have aged overnight after retiring — because they haven't been active — and others who look rejuvenated as though they have taken 10 or 15 years back from history.

Stay Physically Active

If you want to enjoy your retirement to the fullest, stay healthy and active as long as you can. There is nothing better than exercise to help get the body going. Exercise plays a significant role in a retiree's lifestyle. The fact is, getting up in the morning to complete an exercise routine gives an immediate purpose to your day and sets you up for feeling great all day. It's been proven that exercise in the morning helps keep you a little bit sharper throughout the day. It also leads to getting the proper amount of rest. What that exercise is will depend on your level of health and mobility. It could be as simple as a walk or some sort of yoga or other cardiovascular workout. If mobility is an issue, check out your local recreation center's schedule for water or chair aerobics. You may not be taking laps around the track the way you did in your years prior to retirement, but you're still moving. Remember, this is about your optimal health — retired or not.

Stay Digitally Current

Technology moves faster and faster these days, and our connected world relies on digital literacy to survive. It's important for retirees to stay current on technology in order to stay independent and fully engaged with their local community and broader society. Learning a new skill also keeps your brain sharp and healthy. Sign up for computer classes at your local library, make regular appointments with the "geniuses" at the Apple Store and take advantage of their free classes, or invite the grandkids over to tutor you on the latest technology. Whatever it takes to stay connected to the world.

My father-in-law is 80 years old, and he's tech savvy, which I commend. He uses his phone to send texts. He's pretty sharp. Apple offers free classes where he learns how to text and FaceTime and do all this stuff that his grandchildren are doing.

Learn New Skills

There's a saying that the brain doesn't grow old; it grows rust. It's clever, but there is also some truth to it. Studies have shown that our brains are healthier when we keep learning new skills throughout our lives. If you want to retain mental acuity into your 80s and 90s, it's a smart idea to keep a list of new skills you'd like to learn or topics you'd like to explore. If you've always been fascinated by ancient European history, attend a course at your local college. Foodies can indulge in culinary classes. Learn about horticulture if you're an avid gardener. Even if you're less physically mobile, you can learn to knit, crochet, paint, or sew. And if you're planning to travel, how about learning a new language for each new destination? All that learning can really help keep the rust off your brain.

Here are six tips to help you enjoy a dignified and meaningful retirement.

1. **Keep an active calendar.** This will include a regular activity, frequent visits to family, trips, grandkids' sports and activities. A full calendar is good for the brain and also gives a sense of satisfaction.

2. **Exercise every day.** A walk in the park or 30 minutes of light calisthenics — you decide how you move. But make a point to move every day.

3. **Stay up on technology**. Learn how to use the latest techniques with your smart device and consistently stay in contact with friends and loved ones. I highly advise that retirees stay involved in technology. (It's also fun.)

4. **Mentor.** You can't imagine the satisfaction of helping someone and watching them grow, professionally, educationally, or even spiritually. There are so many people who could use guidance in many areas, and your wisdom can aid them in their endeavors. It gives you the opportunity to consider someone's life besides your own.

5. **Work on that bucket list.** Whatever is on your list, do as many of them today as possible while you are in the

go-go years. Now that you have the time, plan your trips, inventions, and hobbies, and make sure you get them done.

6. **Eat to live**. You've worked very hard to get to the place you are now, so why not refocus that dedication toward your health? The object of the game is to enjoy retirement and stay healthy to do the things you want to do for as long as you can.

I had a client win the lottery. True story. Instead of running out and getting a Rolls Royce or a bigger house, the first thing they did was hire a chef and remodel their kitchen. Their meals were pre-made, and there wasn't any chance for them to go off course and start engaging in unhealthy behavior that would ultimately shorten their retirement. The reason for that was to make sure that they stayed fit and trim.

Whether you hit the lottery or not, it makes sense in retirement to change your lifestyle, perhaps eat more healthily, and continue to be the best, healthiest "you" there is.

These are the habits that I think are great disciplines to create a productive and energetic retirement. They give you a successful and dignified retirement so you can live without any regrets and give yourself the best chance of success.

[Exercise:]

① Follow the traits of successful retirees.

② Make the right preparations.

Chapter 4

Establishing Your Family Legacy

"If you would not be forgotten as soon as you are dead, either write something worth reading or do something worth writing."

Benjamin Franklin

We often think of a legacy as the amount of money we leave behind in trust or a will to the next generation. But I'd like to challenge you a bit to think about the nonfinancial legacy you will leave. It may be more valuable than any financial gain a person can inherit. Are there life lessons you want to hand down to the younger generation? Are there experiences you want your children or grandchildren to have and treasure throughout their lives?

After a lifetime of working with retirees, I can tell you that I believe what is important in life is the impact one impresses upon the lives after them. I want my great-grandkids to know about my life and my accomplishments. You may be thinking this about your own life as well.

It's not about money; it's about legacy. Everyone leaves behind a memory after they die that lives in the minds of their surviving loved ones. If you craft your legacy, you'll know those memories are positive, affirming, and profound.

We all work hard for our money to carry that hard-earned money into our retirement to enjoy. Yet, this is not our legacy. Whether you have $8 million, $800,000, or $8,000 in the bank, your legacy is still important.

Building a legacy also doesn't mean that you give as much money to your family first in your will. In many ways, leaving money is the easiest part. I think there's another way of looking at a family legacy. Who are the family members to whom you'd want to give some special recognition? When I say special recognition, I mean they did something worth being remembered.

My grandmother was in the "Guinness Book of World Records" for a long time because she taught the same grade in the same classroom for something like 50 years. If Ross Perot hadn't changed the law in Texas, she would have still been there. What an incredible legacy to be in the "Guinness Book of World Records" for something she did with academics.

Telling your family stories to the younger generation keeps the memories of loved ones alive long after they've passed. This is a legacy you can give to your own parents or other past relatives, a legacy you bestow upon the next generation to cherish and add on to throughout their own lives.

Create a Family Mission Statement

What I mean by mission statement is: What is the belief system that you really want to share with your family? With my own family, it is a priority that we help people. Our family has always been lucky to have good friends around us who, through thick and thin, have been able to help us, not only financially but in other ways as well. I want that tradition of kindness and helping others in need to continue, taught from one generation to another. When you have the money, it's easy to write a check and be ambivalent, not even knowing what the money you are handing out is for. But to actually dedicate focused and directed help for someone that's truly in need is life changing. I continue this tradition because I want my kids to experience that feeling.

When my son was 5 years old, he and I were in New York City, and a homeless person approached him. "Can I have some money for a meal?" the man asked. My son looked at me and said, "Dad, that man looks hungry. I'd like to do it." I gave him $5 and said, "That'd be great. You offer him the $5 and tell him what you're doing." My son said to him, "Here's $5. I hope you can get a nice meal." To me, that was a meaningful exchange for a 5-year-old to experience.

Now, I certainly knew, because I worked in New York, that this person asked for money every day, and I'm not sure if it went to food, but that was beside the point. My son experienced empathy and responded with generosity. That lesson for my son was well worth it.

My daughter has seen all her life that, to our family, money is not something to be flaunted. It's about having the ability to do things with and for family and friends. It's never about making someone feel uncomfortable because they have less. It's about sharing what we have — even if it's a small thing, like a meal or a coffee. My daughter treats her friends to Starbucks every now and then, knowing that some of them cannot afford it otherwise. I think that's a wonderful thing. Instead of making her friends feel bad because they cannot go, she's happy to put it on her app and treat, and I love that about her. That's one of our family belief systems.

Your family mission statement should answer a few key questions.

What knowledge will you hand down? Does your family have unofficial mottos that you live by? My grandfather used to say, "If you hang around nine broke people, you're bound to be the tenth." I have never forgotten that statement. I understood what he was saying, which was to choose your crowd the right way; otherwise, you will end up looking just like your crowd.

Where's the wealth in the assets? It's wonderful to leave the assets and the money to future generations, but let's have a conversation on how that wealth was accumulated. What sacrifices were made? What did you do to earn it? What was your job, and what was it like? It's the story of hard work, perseverance, sacrifice, and gained wisdom that is the wealth behind the asset. Be sure to pass that down with the money.

What is the plan? I inherited some real estate years ago, and we quickly put into our plan that the land would stay in the family. When I purchased investments for my children, I told my children to keep the land until they turn at least 30 years old, if they need to sell it at all. The purpose was to keep a family legacy and a potential appreciating asset.

How do you want to be remembered? Have you seen the Disney Pixar movie "Coco"? In it, a young boy named Miguel learns the importance of being remembered by his family. Those in the land of the dead with no family to remember them are forgotten and experience a second death. They vanish completely. It is a powerful story about the importance of family stories and family legacies.

As morbid as it may sound, consider how you want your friends and family to remember you after you're gone. Do you want them to remember you as kind, gentle, generous? Should they recall your amazing cooking, your fantastic piano playing, your artistic aptitude? Talk about how you would like to be remembered.

I try to make light of many situations; I enjoy telling jokes, making people laugh, and making them comfortable. That's something I'd like to be remembered for. Yours is up to you. I think that's something that should be defined in a simple letter.

Your Medical Legacy

I know, I know. This one seems less touchy-feely than the others, but I promise you it is just as important. Your medical record has a profound impact on the health of future generations. You must tell everyone what, if any, medical conditions you may have. It can help the other generations, but most importantly, it could solve a lot of problems. Knowing your family medical history can be preventative for future generations.

We lost a very good family friend, and one of the regrets his spouse had was that she never had an autopsy done. For years, there's been speculation about what caused his death. Maybe it was an aneurism; maybe it was a heart condition. Who knows? Fast-forward to today, when there are grandchildren and great-grandchildren, it would have been nice to know that information.

Remember that you're not putting yourself first; you're putting other generations first. We've seen people who don't talk about medical conditions or ailing diseases because they are embarrassed or ashamed. If that is you, I hope my story helps you overcome this.

My mother has bipolar disorder.

Now doctors can debate whether it's hereditary or not, but it's important to know moving forward to watch for that type of behavior in myself or my children. They need to know that their grandmother has bipolar disorder — because ultimately, we're trying to help the next generation.

When we think about establishing a family legacy, these are the topics that should be considered. Writing it down solidifies it. It gives you a consensus. But even if you don't write it down, I think what's most important is sharing those ideas — letting future generations have something to reference as they grow up and experience their own journeys.

I look at my children … and wonder how time has gone by so quickly. I can remember my son walking off to kindergarten, and I had to fight back my tears. I thought, *Let me just run to the car so no one can see me crying because we can't have a big football player crying.* It's like all you care about is just making sure they're okay. It's such a hard thing to do when you're thinking about the family. Planning your retirement and creating a meaningful legacy is one more part of that.

The True Definition of Wealth

I think the richest people in the world aren't the Kardashians or the Kennedys with all their money. The richest people are those that are 25-deep at Thanksgiving. A family reunion of 125 people from 12 different states. That's wealth.

My father-in-law's 81st birthday was in 2020, and I can tell you he has 20 or 25 more birthdays at best. Who am I not to just enjoy the day, enjoy the time? (My father didn't have his 74th birthday.) He will be surrounded by his big, extended family and good friends. That's wealth. That's what matters in the end.

A Family Legacy is Family First

A family legacy is not just about money, documents, and assets. In many ways, that is the easy part of a legacy. Consider the following questions when establishing a family legacy.

Who are the family members to whom you want to give special recognition? These members could be war heroes, celebrities, government officials, or anyone who has sacrificed to help the family get to their place today. Tell their stories. Make sure they are remembered.

What is your family mission statement? This is a belief system that will encompass your family values, beliefs, and even sayings to be passed down to future generations.

Where are the wealth and assets? It is wonderful to leave assets and money to our future generations, but it is just as wonderful to leave lessons on how this money was accumulated and the value and wisdom of how to keep it for generations.

How do you want to be remembered? Write some facts that you would love future generations to know. Express some hidden talents or interests that family members may forget.

What is your medical history? Your medical records will have a profound impact on the health of future generations in your family.

Leaving a legacy leaves a powerful message to others, whether it's a financial legacy or it's just in passing down brainpower and family stories. It really is a stamp of approval and fulfillment of your lifelong work to leave some sort of legacy and help generations after you. Think about your legacy, how you want to be remembered, and what impact you would like your life to make on the future. Most retirees would agree they would like to leave this earth better for their children than themselves. Your legacy can help make that possible.

Chapter 5

Emotional Investing

It isn't stress that makes us fall—it's how we respond to stressful events.

Wayde Goodall

We are all emotional about our money, but for financial advisors, our role is to offer unemotional advice and counsel based on training, experience, and wisdom. Here is a chart that shows all the emotions in a traditional mind.

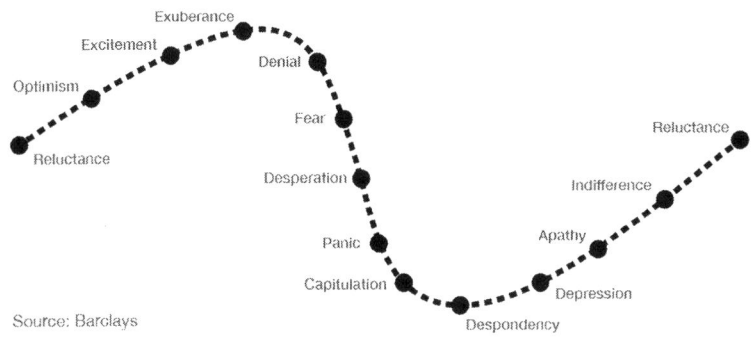

The Casino Story

Allow me to share with you "the casino story." Emotional investing is like being at a craps table. Everyone's yelling and screaming, so we run over to the table because we want to be included in the hoopla. Why is it that we get involved in the stock market when things are high? Because everyone's making money, and we don't want to be left out. As soon as things don't go well, when someone rolls a seven on a craps table, a lot of people leave. As soon as the stock market goes the other way, we sell and get out.

If you can control the emotional side of investing and stay disciplined — that discipline may be simply knowing how long you're invested for — then you will position yourself well in retirement. Having a timeline is a great start.

Say to yourself:

"It doesn't matter what happens with the day-to-day ups and downs of the stock market. I know I'm in this for 25 years."

or

"I know this particular bit of money is going to be left to my children, so I don't have to worry about trading it every day."

or

"I've come with a certain amount of money that I am prepared to lose, so I'm not going to panic. When the first "seven" comes up, I'm not just going to get up and leave. I'm also not going to put all my eggs in one basket."

Unfortunately, when you think about the emotions of investing, people tend to want too much of one thing and pile on, and it creates a herd mentality. Fear of missing out generates anxiety, and the risk of losing money creates anxiety, so there is a yo-yo of positive and negative anxiety dictating your investing. That's not a strategy, and it typically doesn't go well.

Purchasing with Emotions

Emotional connections can cause you to justify the purchase of almost anything. Think of a big purchase, like a home. Builders are famous for this. There's a reason why they stage a model home. The model is basically showing you the life that you want to live. You're never going to see a home model or showroom with a jar of peanut butter on the counter or dishes in the sink or a garbage can full of dirty Pampers, which is more like real life. Instead, what is staged for you is the perfect scene from the life you want. What you see is a pristine home; it's got every upgrade you can possibly imagine — the best appliances, and nothing is ever dirty.

As you walk through the model, you start to justify how you can achieve this perfection. Even if it's too expensive, you may decide that you're going to do whatever it takes to make that home purchase happen, all because you are wowed by the staging of the home model. Then, you move into this home, and the crown molding isn't there, the appliances aren't there — all the things that you thought you were going to have aren't there — but you've made all these sacrifices just to get into your "dream home."

Then you figure out later on, after the shine wears, that maybe this isn't as exciting as you originally had conceived.

Even worse, maybe you didn't plan for the car to break down. Maybe you didn't plan for the extras you would need to put into this home. That's what happens with emotional purchases. People experience it all the time.

The condo industry in Florida was famous for it. They would give you some champagne, talk to you about all the wonderful amenities, and get you to sign on the dotted line, but there was one thing people forgot. When you buy something out of state, you're not going there every week. At the time, it feels like you're going to fly down there all the time, but you're not.

Sometimes it's better to come back and look at it practically. Car dealers do the same thing. The new car smell, the shiny showroom, the test drive — it's all designed to trigger your emotional responses. I'm not saying any of these things are bad; I'm just saying it's amazing how emotions compel us to have specific reactions and make certain purchases.

Emotions are great, but you can't let them rule your retirement strategy. You can't just decide that because there's a new administration in the White House, you're going to sell everything — because those losses may be for a lifetime. You also can't delude yourself into thinking you'll work forever or panic when the stock market has a bad week. You have to look at retirement with your eyes wide open and the logical side of your brain dialed up to 11. It's essential to decide what's important and what you can truly control. Taxes, interest rates, the stock market, and the economy are all important, but you can't actually control any of it. What you can do is take steps to plan and mitigate some of the risks those items pose.

You *can* decide what your risk tolerance is. If you're worried about the stock market going up and down, figure out how much you can risk. You *can* decide how to respond to changes in interest rates. Maybe you lock in a low mortgage rate, reduce credit card debt, or decide to pay off some debt because you know rates are going higher.

If you know federal income taxes are going to create a problem, and it looks like taxes are continuing to go up, then there are ways you *can* mitigate that risk — maybe by owning a home where property taxes are not so expensive or even moving to a state without income taxes.

Or better yet, there may be some other options where you're putting some of your money toward a Roth IRA option, which gives you the ability to pay taxes today and let the investment grow. In simple terms, you're paying taxes on the seed instead of paying taxes on the harvest.

Those are some of the things you can actually control or plan for if you can't totally control.

Determining what you need to care about as well as what you can change — or perhaps, more importantly, what you cannot — is a helpful way to control emotional reactions. You need to care about taxes, for example, because you need to pay them, but you can't control them. So, take ownership of your responsibility to pay them, but don't agonize over them because you can't control the outcome.

The Anxiety-Control Checklist

Taxes

> Should we care? Yes
>
> Can we control? No

Stock Market

> Should we care? Yes
>
> Can we control? No

Inflation

> Should we care? Yes
>
> Can we control? No

The Economy

> Should we care? Yes
>
> Can we control? No

Interest Rates

> Should we care? Yes
>
> Can we control? No

Personal Budget

Should we care? Yes

Can we control? Yes

So, which one should we spend the most time thinking about? The one that we can control.

What we can do is build smart, proactive plans that take these forces into account. So let's think about it. Can we plan for tax increases by adding a Roth component to our retirement? Or plan for stock market volatility by establishing our risk tolerance and segmenting our long-term investments? Or plan for a bad economy by keeping a 24-month emergency fund and plan for a rise in interest rates by refinancing our homes or paying off our credit card debt?

If you can control your emotional responses to retirement, change, and financial investing, you can save yourself a lot of headaches. You may also save more money (if you pull out of the stock market in a panic, you lose the future value of your investment).

This kind of rational, big-picture, long-term thinking is one of —if not the biggest — benefits of enlisting the help of a financial advisor.

Reduce the Anxiety

Despite all the education and sound financial advice people receive, studies indicate that behavior — including investment behavior — will continue to be driven by emotions. I advise people like this: Don't take out money thinking you'll make a lot more without also acknowledging the risk of losing it all. Find out where your comfort zone is and block out the noise. Do not look at your investments every single day. Read or watch the news if you want, but don't allow a fear-driven rant for ratings sway you to change your strategy. Stay disciplined and monitor your investments, but don't change all your investments because you've read some news. Acknowledge your fears or anxiety, and then move on. Stick to your plan.

Look at past data, especially the U.S. stock market. It's also healthy to look at what has happened after every crash. Traditionally, you'll find out the market has played very well after a downturn. If you're in a long-term position, the best advice is to sit back and wait.

Stock market crashes are scary. Even the words we use around a downturn — "crash," "tank," "depression" — induce fear and anxiety. But a stock market fall is only scary if you don't have sufficient background knowledge. If you can look back at history, you can rest assured that this crash (like every crash that came before it) is most likely going to be temporary and precede a period of greater recovery and growth. Most of the stock market crashes we've seen — 2008 and 2009 and the tech bubble in 1987 and 2000 — were terrible for people, but had individuals stayed the course, they would have made their money back and then some.

Past performance is no indication of future results. There's no guarantee that we won't have to face another Great Depression someday, but if your investments are part of a long-term plan rather than a get-rich-quick scheme, you are less likely to worry about a bad day on the market. You can take the long view and wait.

Reduce Your Debt

One of the best ways to reduce anxiety around retirement is to reduce your debt. Minimum payments, interest rates, and monthly payments can all work against your sense of empowerment when thinking about your retirement. If you have a lot of debt, investing in stocks and bonds can feel risky, maybe even *too risky*. (We'll discuss risk tolerance in greater detail in the next chapter.) But, if you have a plan to pay down your debt that doesn't involve using your stock dividends, then you can focus on paying down your debt while your investments do their thing for the next few years. If you're taking your rent money and buying a stock, you're putting your home at risk. I like stocks, but it's pretty easy to see that this is too much risk. You can't afford to lose that money.

Set Realistic Expectations

Your initial step will be to write down what your expectations are. Repeat them to yourself so that you can hear them out loud, and they begin to make sense to you. If you invest $10,000 and make a 10 percent return, which is a great return, you're going to make $1,000. A $10,000 investment at 10 percent does not make you $200,000. That would actually be a 1900 percent increase and is pretty much impossible. I mention it here because if you're not familiar with investing, your expectations may be unrealistic. To make $200,000 from $10,000 at a 10 percent return (which, again, is a *great* return) would take a decade or more.

The average retiree is always going to be emotional about their investments and emotional about their money. This is the biggest value of working with a financial advisor — they do not operate on emotion and can counter your anxiety with logic and historical data. An advisor serves as a sounding board to take the emotion out of financial decisions.

Choosing an Advisor

The stock market moves up and down based on emotions. Certainly, supply and demand, global supply chains, and other external factors play a part, but the emotions have a scary amount of power over the market. When bad news is reported, people make a sudden decision to pull and dump all their stock. That's the reason why the average investor will continue to buy high and sell low. They're letting their emotions get in the way without actually looking at it from a clear head.

Your advisor is like your own personal Jiminy Cricket, reminding you to "play it safe" and stay on the path toward your goals. And just like investing, if the stock market is going up and all your friends are investing, it's not wrong to look at it and just consider it, but before you make a move, you need to talk with your advisor — somebody who understands the plan that you have for retirement. Emotions can cause us to deviate from a plan, and most of the time, that results in a net loss.

Don't be an emotional investor!

Human nature is certainly hard-wired to be emotional about our money. Money keeps us and our families fed, housed, and clothed, not to mention entertained. When we think about having more money, we often think of how we'd spend it on improving our lives or the lives of our families. We're emotional about our families; we're emotional about our money. That's why we hire a professional. A professional advisor is hired to give you good counsel and advice but also to take the emotion out of money and establish a disciplined process. When you have ideas or fears, an advisor gives you a trusted resource, someone to turn to, talk to, and trust. They become a good steward of your money. An advisor also provides you another layer of protection to prevent impulsive decisions and protect you against actions that could cause lifetime damage to a portfolio.

But before you put your money on the table, you need to be talking with somebody who understands the game.

The value of having an advisor is having a reliable third party, an uninvolved perspective that brings clarity in a moment of chaos. A good advisor can provide sound guidance and take the emotion out of a very complex situation.

When hiring an advisor, the number one objective is to find someone you can trust and spend time with. You want to be able to ask any necessary questions regarding the planning process to give you financial confidence without fear of judgment or bad information. This advisor is trained to take the emotion out of investing and make decisions based only on the facts.

If you're thinking, *my best friend/cousin/sister-in-law/other acquaintance is really good with money, and they'll be my advisor,* you need to think again. Remember, an advisor is both an impartial party to your finances and a trained, licensed professional. If you don't take their advice, will they be angry? Worse, if you do take their advice and it turns out to be not great, will your relationship survive? Mix money and family (or friends) at your risk.

Another mistake retirees make is believing that they can manage their own investments because they watch Fox News or read The Wall Street Journal or articles on The Motley Fool. It's impossible to be impartial about your own finances, and unless you have been paying attention to the financial industry for the last 20 years — I mean, *really* paying attention — you probably don't have the same level of expertise and background knowledge that a financial advisor does.

Financial Advisor Checklist

- Look into their licenses. They must have at least a Series 6 or Series 7 license.

- Check the Financial Industry Regulatory Authority's website for any disciplinary actions.

- Examine the payment schedule. Are they being paid a flat fee or on commission?

- Ask for a sample contract. Read it very carefully.

- Look into their qualifications. Ask for them and review them.

- Are they a good fit for you? Do you get a good feeling? Do they listen to your concerns, answer your questions, and remember details about your life or retirement goals?

[Exercise]

① Choose an advisor that understands your goals.

② Ask the right questions.

Chapter 6

Risk Tolerance

"This way, if there are any problems, all the retirement money isn't at risk."

Ed Slott

Let's start by defining risk tolerance and why an understanding of it is necessary within the context of retirement planning. Risk tolerance is the amount of uncertainty a person can tolerate through the ups and downs of a portfolio balance and investment returns. Understanding risk tolerance also means understanding its two phases:

1) Accumulation phase

2) Distribution phase

In the **accumulation phase,** most investors are worried about returns, balances, and outcomes. Put more simply: How should I save? How much should I save? And where should my retirement funds be? In the **distribution phase** (retired), most retirees have gone from accumulating wealth to a desire for predictable income. Traditionally, risk tolerance changes with age, meaning that the older you are, the less likely you will be comfortable with large fluctuations in your portfolio.

The Accumulation Phase

During the accumulation phase, you are working and putting away money for retirement. You can accept a little bit more risk because if you lose money, you have the working capital to offset that loss. You continue to fill up the retirement bucket with your 401(k) contributions and your other assets because you're working.

But the decumulation or distribution phases is a different animal. You go from building up a cash position and carefully monitoring how your balances and assets are growing to looking for the reliability and predictability of income. As mentioned in the earlier chapters, my happiest clients are those who have their basic needs paid for through pensionizing their retirement dollars.

Risk Tolerance Isn't All About the Outcome

Just because a financial newscaster or journalist says you should be comfortable with a big risk doesn't mean you have to be. You should define your level of comfort when it comes to financial risks. (That said, if you have investments that are keeping you up at night, they are probably not good investments.)

When I was a kid, I learned how to ski with a kid named Steven C. I had never skied before, but I was a high-performing athlete and up for a challenge. My first time on the snow, we got off the lift with no problems and I asked Steven, "What is the name of the hill we're going to ski?"

"It's a black diamond," he said.

"All right. What does that mean?" I asked.

And he said, "Well, that's just the name."

If any of you are skiers, you know that a "black diamond" is not just the name of the hill. I figured that out when we reached the top. The slope was called Zero G, and within 100 yards, I was faced with the steepest hill I have ever seen in my life.

I was terrified.

My heart was pounding. I kept thinking: *I am going to die. I am going to die.* I snowplowed from side to side, picked up speed, avoided a few skiers and within a few minutes had made it down the hill. Amazingly, without a single fall.

Steve came down the hill, and the first thing he said to me was, "Let's go back up and do it again. You made it!"

I grabbed Steve by the collar and told him to never do that to me again. I wasn't prepared for the risk, and I didn't enjoy it.

The same logic applies to your investments. As a retiree, you may not want big swings up or down. Volatility in your investments may feel like an unwelcome risk, whether you make money or not.

Designing Portfolios for Risk Tolerance

When I design portfolios for clients, I like to pensionize the portfolio, giving them as much guaranteed income as possible. Doing so can actually increase their risk capacity without necessarily increasing their risk tolerance. Risk capacity isn't emotional or personal; it's a math equation. Risk capacity is how much risk you can take before it affects your financial goals. Risk tolerance, as I've said before, is very personalized. It's up to the individuals to decide what they want to do in retirement and how much risk they are willing to take to achieve their goals. Traditionally, clients become more conservative as they grow older. Retirees tend to preserve their principal, because there is a big difference between accumulation during working years and distribution in the retirement years.

When determining your level of risk capacity and risk tolerance —remember they are two different things — here are some factors to consider:

- Diversification is key to a successful portfolio.

- Diversification is not just a separation between stocks and bonds.

- Investing always comes with some level of risk. Ask yourself what would happen if any parts of your retirement portfolio evaporated.

- The best-laid plans include a worst-case-scenario foundation. Consider how you would protect yourself from the stock market, healthcare expenses, and a downturn in the economy.

In the distribution years, human capital is depleted or certainly reduced. Many clients do not want to lose principal. They want reliability, safety—an even and uneventful ride.

That's more of a bunny slope than a black diamond. And that's okay. You don't have to take on the biggest risk to reach your financial goals in retirement. Remember, going up a mountain requires a very different mindset than coming down a mountain.

The same thought process applies to retirement. You'll find that if you are not prepared for the risk (or you end up taking on more risk than you wanted to), it can create some health problems, both physical and mental, and also some financial problems.

Investment Types and Risks

The difference between risk capacity and risk tolerance is that while a person may have the capacity to handle a large amount of risk, they may not have the stomach (tolerance) for it. (Remember my example of skiing on the black diamond hill?) Guaranteed income can increase the capacity for risk, but not necessarily the tolerance. You need to determine what your true risk tolerance will be. Can you accept a loss of principal? Can you deal with volatility in the portfolio balances? Try risk tolerance questions and verbalize your risk tolerance to your advisor. Risk is a mindset that is unique to you and your own financial comfort.

Risk Tolerance Questions

1. What is your age?

2. When do you plan to retire, or have you already retired?

3. What is your current debt-to-savings ratio?

4. What is your net worth?

5. How much experience do you have with investing?

6. Do you enjoy other risk-associated activities, or do you prefer consistency and calm?

7. How much financial news do you consume daily, on average?

8. How do you react to negative events or news in your life?

9. Have you prepared for a worst-case-scenario, like a depression or catastrophic health event?

10. What does your retirement money mean to you?

Investing involves risks, including the potential loss of principal. No strategy or product can assure success or entirely protect against loss. Let's review the different types of investments you may choose and their associated risks.

Stocks

Stocks historically have produced long-term gains that are bigger than those of any other asset class. According to Morningstar, from 1926 to 2017, large stocks returned an average of 10 percent per year, including reinvestment of income. What's more, large stocks didn't lose ground during any period of 20 years or longer during that time. Those qualities may make stocks much more appealing for long-term savings than Treasury bonds (which have had about 5.5 percent average annual gains since 1926) or stashing cash under your mattress. Potential returns give stocks the best chance to beat inflation over long periods. That's why they're an essential part of a good retirement portfolio.

Risk

Stocks carry a much greater risk of short-term losses than bonds or cash (the other two major asset classes). Since World War II, Wall Street has endured six bear markets — defined as a sustained decline of more than 20 percent in the value of the S&P 500, according to Fox Business. As a result, it's generally not a good idea to invest a big chunk of money in stocks if you'll need to spend the money within five years or so.

Bonds

Bonds pay interest regularly, so they help generate a steady, predictable stream of income from your savings. This provides the security you need in a market that fluctuates minute by minute. Short-term bonds can be a good place to park an emergency fund or money you'll need relatively soon.

Bonds might not provide as much bang as stocks, but they are an essential part of everyone's retirement portfolio. Here are some of the benefits they can provide:

Stability. Bonds are less likely to lose money than stocks. So buying bonds *and* stocks can reduce your portfolio's losses during stock market declines.

Income. Bonds pay interest regularly, so they can help generate a steady, predictable stream of income from your savings.

Security. Next to cash, U.S. Treasuries provide the least amount of risk while remaining the most liquid investments on the planet.

Tax savings. Certain bonds provide tax-free income. These bonds usually pay lower yields than comparable taxable bonds but may provide higher after-tax income to investors in high tax brackets.

Risk

However, as with everything in life — especially when it involves money — there are risks. Here are three of the major ones:

Inflation risk. Most bond payments are fixed. But, the prices of the things you need to buy keep going up. The longer a bond's term, the greater the chance that the payout won't keep pace with inflation.

Credit risk. This is the risk: that your bond issuer will be unable to make its payments on time (or at all). U.S. Treasury bonds are considered to have virtually no credit risk, while high-yield, or "junk," bonds — issued by companies with weak finances — have high credit risk.

Interest rate risk. Though a bond's life span and interest payments are fixed, thus the term "fixed-income" investment, its overall return can vary based on changes in the economy and the markets. Bonds are traded just like stocks, so changes in the economy or the markets can cause bond prices to rise or fall. Bond prices move in the opposite direction of interest rates: When rates rise, bond prices fall. The longer the term of the bond, the greater the price fluctuation that results from any change in interest rates. (Note that price fluctuations matter only if you intend to sell a bond before maturity or if you invest in a bond fund whose manager trades regularly.)

ETFs

Exchange-traded funds, or ETFs, were invented to combine the simplicity and lower costs of index mutual funds with the flexibility of individual stocks. Unlike most mutual funds, ETFs trade on exchanges, where you can buy and sell them anytime the market is open. With ETFs, you can track broad market indexes, such as the S&P 500, gaining instant diversification. You can pay low fees. And you don't get hit with a tax bill (most of the time) until you sell.

Risk

An investment in ETFs, structured as a mutual fund or unit investment trust, involves the risk of losing money and should be considered as part of an overall, not a complete, investment program. An investment in ETFs involves additional potential risks, including lack of diversification, price volatility, competitive industry pressure, international political and economic developments, possible trading halts, and index tracking error. There is also a risk in sector and specialty ETFs.

Alternative Investments

Investors tend to look for asset classes that are noncorrelated to the stock and bond markets. These are called *alternative investments*. These assets include private equity, hedge funds, managed futures, real estate, commodities, metals, and collectibles, to name a few. Investing in alternative investments may not be suitable for all investors and involves special risks, such as principal losses, potential adverse market forces, regulatory changes, and potential illiquidity. With alternative investments, there is no assurance you will attain the investment objective.

Risk-averse investors must understand the liquidity and distribution of alternative investments. Nonliquid assets can be a part of a well-balanced retirement income plan but should never be all of the retirement income plan, no matter what the distribution rate or dividend.

REIT

A REIT, or a real estate investment trust, is a company that owns, operates, or finances income-producing real estate. This is often done by pooling investors' money to buy and possibly manage commercial or residential buildings. The company then collects rent from its tenants and passes that income onto investors in the form of strong dividends.

How REITs Work

To qualify as a REIT, companies must meet certain guidelines set by Congress. In short, the company must:

- Be considered a corporation under the IRS revenue code
- Be managed by a board of directors

- Be held by at least 100 shareholders, with no fewer than five holding 50 percent of shares

- Invest at least 75 percent of assets in real estate, cash, or U.S. Treasuries

- Derive at least 75 percent of income from real estate

- Have 95 percent passive income, which is income that doesn't require direct action from the corporation, such as rental payments

- Pay out at least 90 percent of its taxable income to shareholders through dividends

REIT share prices may decline because of adverse developments affecting the real estate industry and real property values. In general, real estate values can be affected by a variety of factors, including supply and demand for properties, the economic health of the country or different regions, and the strength of specific industries that rent properties. REITs often invest in highly leveraged properties. Returns from REITs may trail returns from the overall stock market because they are noncorrelated assets. In addition, changes in interest rates may hurt real estate values or make REIT shares less attractive than other income-producing investments. REITs are also subject to heavy cash flow dependency, defaults by borrowers, and self-liquidation.

Investments and Taxes

Bonds generate income, which may be taxable. Interest on corporate bonds is taxable, but some government bonds may be exempt from certain taxes. For example, Treasuries are free from state and local taxes, but you will owe federal taxes. Municipal bonds, on the other hand, are federal tax-free and may be exempt from state and local taxes if you live in the state that issued them. You can also make your portfolio more tax efficient by taking advantage of certain accounts like IRAs and 401(k) retirement plans. Municipal securities may be subject to the alternative minimum tax, and state and local taxes may apply.

Retirement Lifetime Income

Ask yourself this question: At what income do I want to retire?

There are two primary factors in determining how much you can withdraw each year in retirement. How much of your current spending is discretionary versus fixed? And how much of your portfolio is in some sort of guaranteed income product like a pension, annuity, or Social Security?

This is why it is imperative for you to build an income floor. We cannot predict how long we will live, our total retirement outflow, or our investment returns. In many ways, a good advisor should be very conservative with his projections for investment returns and overstate costs and expenses during retirement. As the old saying goes: *A pinch of prevention is worth a pound of cure.* Or, more simply: *It's better to be safe than sorry.*

Setting up an income floor means we first project out the expense for basic needs such as utilities, food, clothing, and housing. We then determine what income will be available through pensions, Social Security, and annuities. We set the lowest possible amount your investments would need to deliver in order to have all of your basic needs met. Lifetime income takes the guesswork out of basic essentials. Lifetime income can prove its value when markets or assets become volatile or even lose value.

[Exercise]

① What are my basic needs, and how do I cover my expenses without worry?

② Create your monthly retirement lifestyle budget.

Chapter 7

Critical Pieces of Your Retirement

"You don't buy insurance because you know when you are going to die or something bad will happen. You buy insurance because we don't know when we are going to die or something bad will happen."

Stephen Oliver

Housing, income, insurance, and healthcare are critical aspects of retirement planning. In this chapter, we'll explore each of these in detail.

Insurance

Most people are familiar with health, home, auto, and, certainly, property insurance, but there are three other very important insurances. Of the five critical pieces to effective retirement planning, there are three types of insurances that you should set in place before and during retirement.

Disability Insurance

In your 50s and 60s, continuing to produce income is critical to your retirement plan. Medical issues and extended health problems are becoming the largest causes of financial disruption, which is why disability insurance is so important. Disability insurance is a safety net that can keep cash flow stable if you cannot work. Policies typically will only cover a portion of your income — about 60 to 70 percent on average, but this can still make a huge difference in your ability to stay on track.

Having a good disability policy will help build and preserve your nest egg. It's important to acquire disability insurance *before* you retire, as many insurers will not offer policies to people over the age of 60.

Long-Term Care Insurance

Imagine yourself living your picture-picture retirement: You have money to live on, the house is paid off, and you are enjoying the comfortable lifestyle that you proposed on your whiteboard. One day life throws you a curveball — a bad one. You need assisted living and care. You obviously want quality care, but how will you pay for it? Are you self-insured? Would you qualify for aid? These are the questions and challenges you will face. The question becomes, do you want to complete your retirement plan without addressing a problem that keeps increasing with age? Did you know that the government process for receiving aid is as follows: You must deplete all your assets, and then they will consider you for aid.

What about the legacy? What about the kids and grandkids? Complete your financial plan by addressing a probable need. Most retirees do not want to be a burden on the family, so independence is very important. Provide for some sort of long-term care, so you are not a burden on your family but also preserve the corpus of your wealth that you desire to pass on to our next generation. There are wonderful products that offer a host of benefits to help with this.

I have told many families the best gift you can give your children is long-term care insurance. There is a high probability that most retirees will need some sort of long-term care. Long-term care insurance covers the cost of home care, nurses, and caregivers and offers daily assistance where necessary. There are many products with different benefits, so please take the time to understand the policies. It is vital to ensure your ability to pay the premiums when you are no longer working and are on a fixed income. If you are wealthy, there is always the option of self-insurance (the ability to pay for any catastrophic health events), but it will be quite costly. According to the Administration for Community Living, an agency of the U.S. Department of Health and Human Services, in 2016, the national cost for a semiprivate room in a long-term care facility averaged about $225 per day or $82,000 a year, with an average stay of 835 days. Long-term care insurance can remove a financial burden from you or your family.

Life insurance

There are as many opinions about life insurance as there are people. Many people don't understand how to factor life insurance into their overall retirement plan. There are some important considerations you should know. When structured properly, life insurance becomes a valuable asset, not only to your retirement but to your legacy. As people age, many who previously had life insurance feel that they no longer need it, but that's not what life insurance is for. If you have dependents, life insurance serves as an excellent asset-replacement tool. It could also serve as an equalizer among families expecting an inheritance. Many policies become paid up after a while, so make sure you understand what you have.

In addition, insurance should be reviewed on an annual basis. Beneficiaries should be checked and updated, and evaluations should be made on the different benefits each policy has. Your advisor can give you more relevant information regarding life insurance as you devise your retirement plan.

Medicare

Healthcare costs can be one of the biggest expenses retirees face in retirement. Medicare costs and benefits should be a key part of your budget when planning for retirement. It is very important to have a detailed understanding of your options, including costs and benefits. The vast majority of retirees sign up for traditional Medicare, which consists of Part A for hospital coverage and Part B for doctor visits and outpatient services. Many also purchase Part D for prescription drug coverage. In addition to the above, many choose a Medicare Plan F to limit out-of-pocket medical costs.

So, who can get this benefit? Retirees who paid at least 10 years' worth of payroll taxes get Part A without paying a premium. The other benefits come out of your monthly Social Security benefits. There are some income thresholds. Married couples with incomes over $170,000 pay surcharges on their Parts B and D premiums, which will be deducted from Social Security. For singles, the income cap is $85,000. These current rules can always change with different government administrations.

Retirees that claim Social Security at 65 are automatically enrolled in Parts A and B. Those that decide to delay Social Security and receive delayed retirement credits should sign up during a seven-month enrollment window. This window will be three months before you turn 65, the month you turn 65, or three months after you turn 65. Failing to do so will result in a 10 percent penalty on the Part B premiums for each calendar year without coverage. This will be for the life of the coverage.

Medicare Initial Enrollment Period
(7 months)

Month You Enroll	Month Part B Coverage Begins
1st month	1st day of month you reach age 65
2nd month	1st day of month you reach age 65
3rd month	1st day of month you reach age 65
4th (birthday) month	1st day of following month (1-month delay)
5th month	Two-month delay
6th month	Three-month delay
7th month	Three-month delay

Exception:
If you were born on the 1st day of the month:
- Seven-month IEP begins and ends one month earlier;
- Eligible for Medicare month before reaching age 65.

If you are 65 and working, there is a special eight-month enrollment period that begins when the employer health coverage ends. *Caution: COBRA does not count as a substitute for healthcare coverage, according to Medicare.* In short, waiting to sign up until COBRA runs out will create a penalty for you and your existing healthcare.

Retirees often make the mistake of ignoring Medicare while they are covered by a plan from their former employer, which could also subject them to penalties. Rules vary amongst plans, but as a rule of thumb, Medicare often serves as the primary insurance, and the retirees' insurance serves as a backup or secondary.

Medicare Part A helps for hospital services if you are an inpatient. It also pays for care in a skilled nursing facility or hospice and some home healthcare.

Medicare Part B covers 80 percent of most doctor and outpatient costs such as transplants, surgical consults, laboratory, and medical devices. Wellness visits and mammograms are free. It does not cover the most common issues for seniors: physical therapy and bone density screenings.

Medicare Part D is used for drug coverage. These coverages are from private insurers. These plans vary immensely — from premiums, drugs covered, and out-of-pocket costs. Many drugs are covered, but retirees may have to cover as much as 30 percent of the specialty drugs. Plans change from year to year, so it is important to review and reassess your current coverage.

Medicare Part F is the most comprehensive. This particular plan covers co-pays, deductibles, and coinsurance not covered by Part A and Part B. Policyholders cannot be charged for preexisting conditions.

These policies are only available in a limited number of states. The plan requires you to use hospitals and doctors within its network to be eligible for full insurance benefits. Premiums are generally lower; however, if you do not use the selected hospital or doctor for nonemergency services, you may incur higher costs. Whether or not your Medicare plan pays in full, Medicare will pay its share of approved charges, regardless of which hospital or doctor is chosen.

There are **two ways** to receive Medicare health insurance when you retire: through Medicare Part A and B or through private insurance, such as a Medicare Advantage plan (aka Medicare Part C). Most people become eligible for Medicare health insurance when they turn 65. You may be able to qualify for Medicare at any age if you have an end-stage renal disease requiring dialysis, a kidney transplant, or ALS (Lou Gehrig's) disease. You MUST be an American citizen or permanent legal resident of at least five continuous years.

Medicare Advantage

This is a popular option, but there is a downside or trade-off. It is limited to a network of providers that sometimes doesn't include an academic medical center or specialized cancer facility. This option has also been rumored to deny care. If you plan to be a "snowbird" or travel a lot in retirement, this may not be the best plan for you because of the restrictive nature. One good thing is these plans have a premium of zero, so there is no out-of-pocket cost.

Four Steps to Buying a Policy

1. Decide which benefits are needed and choose the standardized Medigap policy that best meets those needs.

2. Find out which insurance companies sell Medigap policies in your state.

3. Write down and review the cost and options information for each plan.

4. Select and purchase your Medigap policy in a timely manner.

For more information, visit Medicare.gov.

Housing in Retirement

Housing plays a major part in your retirement plan. If you own your own home, should you stay in it throughout your retirement? Should you rent or buy? Downsize, upsize, or just-the-right size? There are so many questions that revolve around housing.

You could sell your home so as to not deal with the hassle of taking care of yourself and an aging home. Then the question is, should you rent or buy? Renting sounds wonderful, but remember, you are on a fixed income, and rents tend to increase. When you rent, there is no equity buildup. It is recommended that seniors spend no more than 15 percent of their annual retirement income on housing, whether renting or owning.

Mortgages

So, should you have a mortgage in retirement? Some financial professionals would answer with a resounding "No." They look at it in terms of net returns. Imagine you have $100,000 socked away. You could use that money to pay off your mortgage or keep it invested in the stock market. Say your mortgage interest rate is 4 percent. The pros will tell you to hang on to the mortgage because you may net 8 percent of gains from the stock market, putting you ahead 4 percent overall.

In most cases, mortgages should not be paid off with retirement assets or emergency funds. The truth is, Americans have a love-hate relationship with mortgages, and with good reason. While these long-term loans have allowed folks across the socio-economic strata an avenue to homeownership, the mortgage is also perhaps the most dreaded bill we pay every month. Why? Because it is by far our biggest monthly expense.

Depending on individual circumstances, I advise my clients to pay off their mortgage if they can before retirement, without dipping into their retirement savings. There are wonderful advantages to paying off your largest asset:

1. You can always remortgage.

2.   You can take a home equity line of credit (HELOC).

3.   You may transfer the home to your heirs.

If you don't have tens of thousands of dollars to drop on your mortgage, that's perfectly okay. And you're not alone – very few people can throw a substantial amount of money at their house payment all at once. Most happy retirees who own their homes outright paid off their mortgages early, little by little, making more than the minimum monthly payment over several years. In my experience, probably 70 percent of retirees who are mortgage-free used this method to reach that goal.

Downsizing

Downsizing in retirement could be a wonderful way to inject cash into the retirement income plan. Selling a family home can be very emotional, and I don't want to dismiss or minimize that. But, with the right mindset, it could be very rewarding. Take time to get rid of unnecessary items. Cleaning a closet can be as rewarding as paying off a debt. Retirees need to have a clean and well-organized home. Cleaning and organizing make life easier in the event of a premature passing. It leaves your heirs with less to manage in deciding which items to keep and which items to throw away.

Estate Planning

There is another critical piece of retirement planning, and that is planning your estate. What will you leave to your family when you die, and how will your belongings be distributed? I've chosen to give this critical piece its own chapter.

Exercise

① What insurance will I need in retirement?

② Where do I want to live and how much house can I handle?

Chapter 8

Estate Planning in Retirement

"It is always wise to look ahead, but difficult to look further than you can see."

Winston Churchill

Many people think that estate planning is only for the extremely wealthy because they are the ones with multiple vacation homes or who live on actual estates. This is not the case. Everyone has an estate — no matter the size. Your estate comprises everything you own — your car, home, other real estate, checking and savings accounts, investments, life insurance, furniture, and personal possessions. Estate planning puts you in control of everything you own; the state you live in doesn't get to do whatever it wants with your possessions. This way, you determine to whom and to where your estate goes.

Do you hear that? It's the refrain of estate planning procrastination. It sounds something like this:

"I'm not going to die tomorrow; I will do it later."
"There is plenty of money, so let them figure it out."
"I don't have enough wealth to need estate planning."

These are common excuses that prohibit people from estate planning. Even folks in their 70s will put off estate planning. Perhaps it feels too final; perhaps folks think if they plan their estate, they might as well get busy dying. Interestingly, it's been my experience that people who have wills live longer than those who don't (certainly not a fact, but it seems to be the case with my clients).

You don't want your children, siblings, and other family members squabbling over your assets after you've gone. Grief combined with ambiguity can lead to devastating conflict at a time when a family should be closest. Estate planning prevents this conflict.

It is amazing, statistically, how many people have not taken care of these issues. According to a 2015 Rocket Lawyer estate-planning survey by Harris Poll, 64 percent of Americans don't have a will. Of those without a will, about 27 percent said there isn't an urgent need for them to make one — and 15 percent said they don't need one at all.

I'm going to be blunt here: Not having a will does not mean you will live forever. Prepared or not, death comes for us all. Avoiding estate planning isn't a magic trick that unlocks immortality. The only thing it unlocks is a lot of confusion and strife for your family after you pass.

I read a story in 2011 in which a man forgot to change the beneficiary on his life insurance after he and his first wife divorced. The man's new spouse was certainly expecting to collect when he passed away, but unfortunately, the beneficiary was still listed as his first wife, whom he had divorced 10 years prior. The Supreme Court favored the ex-spouse (Hillman v. Maretta). Without planning and looking into beneficiaries, it could be a tremendous blow to a financial plan for your surviving spouse or other family members.

You've got to make arrangements for things that are going to be controversial. If you have specific wishes for your funeral, it's imperative that those wishes are put in writing. That's what a good estate plan will do. It may seem morbid, but I recommend that even young people have a basic will and plan. Tragedies are part of our human existence; knowing a person's last wishes can be a small relief to their families after they are gone, perhaps even more so when the person is young or the death unexpected.

When my father passed away, he only told us what he wanted verbally; he put nothing into writing. He said he wanted a closed casket and no flowers or personal stories. He didn't want it to turn into a big deal. Yet, his sisters and brothers thought differently. My brother and I had to fight them, advocating for our father's verbally expressed wishes. We felt we were in the best position to explain it because we lived closer to our father in New Jersey than his siblings in Texas. In the end, everyone agreed to abide by his wishes, but if that wasn't a friendly debate, it could've been very, very messy.

Making arrangements for your final days or even planning your funeral isn't only about helping your family through rough times; it is also about designating representatives to make decisions about your care, money, and the distribution of your assets. Indeed, 70 percent of wealthy families lose their wealth by the second generation, and a stunning 90 percent by a third, according to the Williams Group wealth consultancy.

If you own property in several states, the rules in each state may be different concerning who will be entitled to your properties. Typically, intestate law divides the decedent's estate between the surviving spouse and living children; however, many people are surprised by the actual division made by state law. Even if the decedent does not have children, the spouse generally will not inherit the entire estate.

Critical Documents

Will

A will designates who is going to inherit your property. A will is important because if you do not designate who inherits your property, a state statute will. The statutory distribution scheme (known as "intestate distribution") will often provide results differing from your wishes. How would you feel if some stranger decided to divvy up your estate or even raise your children? Unless you have appointed a guardian for your minor children or executed a legal will, this could happen.

You can find a do-it-yourself website to assist you in your wishes or seek out a qualified trust and estate planner. Make sure they are not a real estate attorney and that their bread and butter is practicing trust and estate.

Don't trust a friend to do this for you. This is not a favor or a nice-to-have. This is one of the most important legal documents of your life. Spend the money to get it right. The more complex your circumstances, the more you need a qualified professional to handle them.

Durable Power of Attorney

This is a document that provides a person you delegate the authority to manage your finances and legal affairs. A power of attorney must be executed when you have capacity but can be used in the event that you become disabled or incapacitated if you specify so. This document allows your loved ones to handle your matters directly in the event of incapacity without going through a lengthy and expensive guardianship proceeding. A power of attorney becomes invalid upon the principal's death. The durable power of attorney will be executed just in case you become incapacitated or disabled. It allows someone you have designated to act on your best behalf.

Healthcare Directive

It is a legal document in which a person specifies what actions should be taken for their health if they are no longer able to make decisions for themselves because of illness or incapacity. This document outlines some of your designated wishes. Think of every tragic news story where a family is torn apart because a loved one is on life support, and nobody knows if they'd want to remain living in that condition or not. Personal preferences and biases take the place of informed decisions. However, you feel about life support, the healthcare directive can take care of that. It can also state whether you prefer to be resuscitated or not in an emergency health event. This document can be invaluable for avoiding family conflicts and possible legal intervention if someone is unable to make a healthcare decision.

Revocable Living Trust

There are many different types of trusts with different purposes, each accomplishing a variety of goals. A revocable living trust is one type of trust often used in an estate plan. Revocable means it could be changed, but it at least gives some sort of structure as to what you would want to be done. By transferring assets into a revocable trust, you can provide for continued management of your financial affairs during your lifetime (when you're incapacitated, for example), at your death, and even for generations to come. Your revocable living trust allows your trust assets to avoid probate and reduces the chance that personal information will become part of public records.

Every revocable trust has three important roles. The grantor or settlor — generally you — creates the trust and transfers assets to it. The beneficiary(ies) — often you and your family — receive the income and/or principal according to your trust's terms. A trustee — who could be you, a family member, or a corporate trustee — manages the trust assets. You can change a revocable trust's provisions at any time during your life. If you act as your own trustee, you continue to manage your investments and financial affairs. In this case, your account might be titled "(Your Name), Trustee of the (Your Name) Revocable Living Trust Dated (Date)."

If there are major changes in your life, like a divorce, loss of a spouse, or loss of a child, your critical documents should be reviewed and updated immediately.

In times of tragedy, conflict, and high emotions, people will have different interpretations of what the deceased was trying to say.

We say in Manhattan, "Why guess when you can know?" If it's put in writing, you know exactly what the person meant. If it's not in writing, then it's up for interpretation. Having all of your critical documents in order years before you retire eliminates the stress and guesswork for your family, and also possible pain and anguish by declaring your wishes and plans clearly.

Protect yourself and your family by making sure you have assistance in estate planning from a licensed professional that specializes in trust and estate planning.

Exercise

① Are your wills up to date?

② Are your beneficiaries up to date?

③ Have there been any changes in your wishes or to your family?

Chapter 9

Your Attitude and the Happiness Recipe

"We don't stop playing because we grow old. We grow old because we stop playing."

George Bernard

The Bernard quote encompasses the symbiotic relationship between your attitude and action and the power of that relationship. Attitude is very important for those approaching and already in retirement. Having a positive attitude toward your future vitally impacts that future.

When you retire, the last thing you want to do is have a negative attitude. I know many retirees who wake up in the morning, and they pray. They're thankful for the day. They look forward to having another day and having the freedom and ability to be in the elite group that is retired. They always try to look at the bright side. Changing your attitude changes your outlook. It's inevitable that as you get older, wrinkles and gray hair will come. Embrace it instead of worrying about it.

A negative attitude says, "I'm going to retire, but I don't have enough money. And I'm not going to have anything to do. I don't like exercise. I don't. I don't. I don't." This negative refrain becomes a self-fulfilling prophecy. You don't exercise, you don't go out, you don't have fun, and you don't enjoy retirement. Why do that to yourself when positive thinking can change it?

Those embracing retirement say, "Yes, I'm older now. I'm 65 (or 67, or 70). I have more gray hairs, but I'm getting wiser and better — like a fine wine." My father-in-law turned 81 while I was writing this book, and he wants to see if he can make it to 100 years old. And that's a great goal to have. The fact of the matter is, he's not sitting back saying, "Well, I'm retired. I've been retired for 15 years. I'm just going to roll up in a cave and not do anything." He has the right attitude, and I believe that when it comes to retirement (and life in general), a positive attitude is just as important as a solid financial plan.

Our belief system can work for us and against us. A successful retirement starts with attitude. The next step is exercise — both mental and physical.

Physical Exercise

Joints stiffen and muscles weaken as we age. It's a fact of life. What should we do about it? Exercise. Whether it's lifting weights, swimming, or yoga, anything to keep the muscles moving and limbs flexing is good for your health. In fact, a study in 2018 showed that people in their 70s who had exercised regularly were healthier than their counterparts who did not exercise. Specifically, their hearts, lungs, and muscles were in equivalent shape to that of a 40-year old[1]. Exercise won't make you young again, but it can help you feel younger for a lot longer.

1 *Source:* Cohut, Maria Ph.D. Medical News Today, "Regular Exercise Can Keep the Body Decades Younger" November 2018.

Exercise also helps your mental health, which we touched on in Chapter 3. Like any major life event, facing retirement can evoke as much anxiety or even dread as it does joy and contentment. Keeping your mind balanced and thinking positively will help you create your perfect retirement. Exercise has been shown to improve memory, mental acuity, and self-esteem while reducing feelings of anxiety and depression. We should all be exercising every day — but if you never have before, retirement is definitely the time to start.

Mental Exercise

There's also mental exercise as well. This was also discussed in Chapter 3. Brain games, skills building, and the stimulation of social situations are all good for your mental acuity and mental outlook. Puzzles, sudoku, crosswords, any of the myriad apps available right now, and even a few hands of cards can improve your outlook and your mental function.

Regular physical and mental exercise will keep your brain sharp and your outlook positive, two things that are almost guaranteed to contribute to a happier retirement and greater fulfillment during your retired years. The best way to go into retirement is with a positive mental attitude. Not being afraid, having a clear cut-plan, and keeping your chin up really does lead to a successful retirement.

Embrace every day and celebrate that you are now a part of an elite group of retirees and have the privilege to pass on your wisdom.

Attitude

What should you do if your attitude toward retirement isn't as positive as you might wish? First off, don't panic or start feeding yourself judgmental or negative thoughts. Lots of people have a conflicted relationship with the idea of retirement. Some fear the loss of professional status, others worry about finances, and some worry about the possibility of becoming a burden to their children later in life. All of their reasons are different, but all of them are equally valid. The important thing is to acknowledge the issue and work toward a solution.

Talking seems to be the best therapy for retirement anxiety or depression. Talk to your partner, your children, and your friends who are already retired. Join groups on social media and read other retiree's stories. If you don't feel ready to share your feelings publicly (or even if you do), writing in a journal can help you process your thoughts and emotions and improve your outlook. Finally, talking to a mental health practitioner and making a plan for your mental health during retirement can ease the transition. Remember, retiring is as big of a life change as getting married or having a child. It's totally normal to have questions, doubts, or concerns. Address them before you retire or early in your retirement so that you can have maximum happiness for the maximum amount of time.

The Happiness Recipe

Add a cup of laughter, a dash of joy, lots of positive attitude, and sprinkles on top, and you just might have a recipe for happiness. Or is there even such a thing?

The theme of this book is that there is more to life than just numbers and having a pile of wealth. There's a secret to it. That secret is what we call the Happiness Recipe. Health, family, and wealth are the secret ingredients to a successful retirement.

I once had a client who wanted to practice retirement. He put himself on a budget and wanted to see what it felt like to restrict his purchases. He did not like the fact that he lost a little bit of control. He said, "This is really hard to be on a fixed income. I don't know if I could do it." He decided to go back to work. He took a consulting gig where he wasn't putting away money but was spending everything he had. Again, it was something that I thought was a good exercise for him. He fell from a $500,000 a year income to l something more along the lines of about $80,000 or $100,000. That's a big gap to make up if you're used to going out all the time and eating out; you're making a total transformation.

That same client planned on downsizing, selling his larger home and buying a smaller one. What he didn't take into account is how much he would spend on renovating the smaller home to suit his desires and needs. He was used to living a certain way and had a hard time adjusting to anything less.

This situation could create a negative perspective on retirement, and that's why practicing is a great idea. Learn what you can and cannot adjust to. What makes you uncomfortable? Is it budgeting on a fixed income or the boredom that comes from being a Type A workaholic who no longer has to go to work? Give yourself a few months as a test run and see how you feel. Don't give up if something seems unbearable. Remember, this is a transition. It will take time to get used to your new life, and a positive attitude makes all the difference.

From what I've been told — because I'm certainly not retired — attitude seems to be the most powerful and critical ingredient in your Happiness Recipe. The goal of this book is to help you achieve your retirement obsession and do it in a way that makes sense and produces the greatest reward.

Chapter 10

Frequently Asked Questions

"The question isn't at what age do I want to retire, it's at what income."

George Foreman

Should I save for retirement or college?

The short answer is *both*. If you can, put a little money aside for your child's college fund and your retirement with each paycheck. Remember that there are prepaid options for college, which can help lock in affordable rates while your child is young. There are also scholarships and grants. Last option, you can always subsidize your college savings with student loans. Be careful, these can hang around and affect your savings later in life, but they are an option. You can't borrow money for retirement, and there are no scholarships for it, either. A creative and well-structured retirement plan may allow you to take some of that money out to fund college if need be. But if you only work on saving for college and not worry about your retirement, it's going to cost you dearly.

How do I reduce my expenses?

Budgeting can sound like a bad word. In order to reduce your expenses, I think the easiest method is to start small. Slowly reduce your spending habits. Look for the smaller balance on loans or credit cards and start to pay those balances off immediately. Pay more on your highest interest rate debts first to knock down those minimum payments. If you have one small debt and one large one, pay off the small one in a lump sum. It's a mental boost to feel like you've made real progress, and it can make paying down the remaining debt feel less arduous. Look for credit cards with points when you're traveling. Points could be a wonderful supplement in retirement. You'll be surprised how many you accumulate if you start early. Airline miles or points are great for visiting family while on a fixed income. You can use your points to pay off these trips or use perks. They can even be used to supplement meals. Many times, our retirees are paying for one meal a day because their credit cards or their points are being used to supplement meals. That's a big savings when you're talking about planning for a vacation or any regular travel.

Should I worry about fees in retirement?

Fees are always a hot topic. Every fee that is charged will impede your ability to make money in your investment count. We're not saying every time you pay a fee, it's a bad thing, but fees in the absence of value are bad. Always look for lower fees if it's something that you're looking at in terms of investment performance. Look for lower fees when it comes to credit cards and any of your financial information. It's just a simple difference of 1 or 2 percent over the course of a 10- or 20-year retirement, and it's a tremendous amount of money that adds up both on credit cards and expenses in the investments.

At pre-retirement, how much should I save each year?

The rule of thumb is about 15 percent (including contributions to a retirement account) of your gross income. Now, if you're not comfortable with 15 percent, let's start off small. If you need to do 5 percent and inch it up 2 percent every year, that's fine. But you would want about 15 percent because ultimately, in a successful retirement plan, you're going to have to replace about 70 percent of your income. That starts by saving early and saving often.

Why is longevity a risk?

Longevity is a risk multiplier of everything — income, health, and care. If you live longer, you must provide for all of the above longer. So you must also understand better ways to take care of yourself. Longevity is a risk multiplier because it increases your worry in retirement about your retirement finances, stock market investments, healthcare out-of-pocket cost, real estate, and fixed income. If you're living longer, everything is magnified by two or three times more. If you're living off a fixed income, you only have a certain amount of money, so if you live an extra 10 years, that creates more pressure. Have you done the proper planning for long-term care? If you continue to live and stay in your home or require assistance, that will also create another concern of longevity.

Conclusion

Today, not tomorrow. Retirement planning is important from a financial perspective and also from an emotional perspective. You will put yourself in the most favorable position if you take action today. Accumulating the funds you need for a comfortable retirement may take decades, depending on your income and your goals, so start NOW. Taking time to identify what is important financially and what is important from a nonfinancial perspective should be discussed and planned immediately. Goals, finances, and health may change, but a good retirement plan will account for all the "what-if" scenarios to provide the best chance for your picture-perfect retirement.

About the Author

Stephen A. Oliver is the founder of Manhattan Ridge Advisors, headquartered in New York City. Manhattan Ridge Advisors is a boutique retirement income planning firm that maintains a client base of pre-retirees and retirees.

Stephen has provided comprehensive wealth management and financial services for over 25 years. In 2005, he founded Manhattan Ridge Advisors. He maintains offices in New York City, Bedminster, and Iselin.

Stephen's practice offers solutions for wealth management, income planning, and retirement services. He is currently a speaker for the "Money Matters" series, an educational campaign underwritten by The McGraw-Hill Company. Stephen has been a member of the Board of Governors for Youth at Risk in New York City and is the former Golf Chairman of New Jersey National Golf Club in Basking Ridge, New Jersey. He currently serves on the Somerset County YMCA board of directors.

Stephen has a passion for education and service excellence in retirement planning and the qualified plan industry. His professional retirement designations include: Retirement Income Certified Professional (RICP®), Chartered Retirement Plans Specialist (CRPS®), Certified 401(k) Professional (C(k)P®), Chartered Retirement Planning Counselor (CRPC®), Accredited Investment

Fiduciary (AIF®), National Social Security Advisor (NSSA®), and the Certified Wealth Strategist (CWS®).

Stephen currently lives in Basking Ridge, New Jersey, and has two children, Stephanie and Christopher. In his spare time, he enjoys coaching wrestling, football, and serving on various community boards.

www.ExpertPress.net

Made in the USA
Middletown, DE
13 February 2021

33718371R00066